Vale of York *and the* Yorkshire Wolds

WALKS

Compiled by
Brian Conduit

Acknowledgements
My thanks for the valuable advice and numerous useful leaflets
that I obtained from the local authorities and the various tourist
information centres throughout the area.

Text:	Brian Conduit
Photography:	Brian Conduit
Editorial:	Ark Creative, Norwich
Design:	Ark Creative, Norwich
Series Consultant:	Brian Conduit

© Jarrold Publishing 2005

OS Ordnance Survey® This product includes mapping data licensed
from Ordnance Survey® with the permission of
the Controller of Her Majesty's Stationery Office. © Crown
Copyright 2005. All rights reserved. Licence number
100017593. Ordnance Survey, the OS symbol and Pathfinder
are registered trademarks and Explorer, Landranger and
Outdoor Leisure are trademarks of the Ordnance Survey, the
national mapping agency of Great Britain.

Jarrold Publishing   ISBN 978-0-7117-2081-7

While every care has been taken to ensure the accuracy of the route
directions, the publishers cannot accept responsibility for errors or
omissions, or for changes in details given. The countryside is not
static: hedges and fences can be removed, field boundaries can
alter, footpaths can be rerouted and changes in ownership can
result in the closure or diversion of some concessionary paths.
Also, paths that are easy and pleasant for walking in fine
conditions may become slippery, muddy and difficult in wet
weather, while stepping stones across rivers and streams may
become impassable.
    If you find an inaccuracy in either the text or maps, please
write to or e-mail Jarrold Publishing at the addresses below.

First published 2002 by Jarrold Publishing
Revised and reprinted 2005

Printed in Belgium. 3/07

Jarrold Publishing
Pathfinder Guides, Healey House, Dene Road, Andover,
Hampshire SP10 2AA
email: info@totalwalking.co.uk
www.totalwalking.co.uk

Front cover: Ripon Cathedral
Previous page: Kirkham Bridge

Contents

Keymaps   4
At-a-glance... walks chart   8
Introduction   10
Walks

1 Danes Dyke and Sewerby   14

2 Hedon   16

3 Wharram Percy   18

4 Boroughbridge and Aldborough   20

5 Lotherton Hall and Aberford   22

6 Humber Estuary   24

7 Kirkham Priory and the River Derwent   26

8 Tockwith and the River Nidd   28

9 Millington Dale   30

10 North Cliff and Filey Brigg   32

11 Ripon and the rivers Shell and Ure   35

12 Howden Marsh and the River Ouse   38

13 Welburn and Castle Howard   40

14 Newbald Wold   42

15 Flamborough Head   44

16 Watton and Kilnwick   47

17 Fridaythorpe and Huggate   50

18 Harpham, Burton Agnes and Kilham   53

19 Sheriff Hutton and Mowthorpe Hill   56

20 Hunmanby, Muston and Stocking Dale   59

21 Londesborough Park and Goodmanham   62

22 Tadcaster and Healaugh   66

23 Hornsea Mere and the Rail Trail   69

24 Nether Poppleton and the River Ouse   73

25 Welton Dale and Brantingham Wold   76

26 Beverley   79

27 Pocklington Canal and Allerthorpe Common   83

28 Thixendale and Kirby Underdale   87

Further Information   90

The National Trust; The Ramblers' Association; Walkers and the Law; Countryside Access Charter; Walking Safety; Useful Organisations; Ordnance Survey Maps

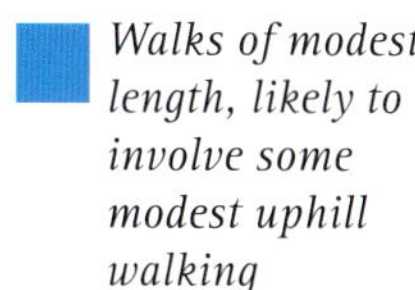

Short, easy walks

Walks of modest length, likely to involve some modest uphill walking

More challenging walks which may be longer and/or over more rugged terrain, often with some stiff climbs

Keymap 1

RIPON
HARROGATE
KNARESBOROUGH
WETHERBY
TADCASTER
LEEDS
GARFORTH
Boroughbridge
Easingwold
Castleford

A61 A1 A168 A19 A59 A661 A64 A58 A6120 A642 A653 A654 A63 A659 A639 A1(M) A1237
M1 M621
B6267 B6265 B6108 B6165 B6164 B6161 B6135 B6157 B6159 B1448 B1224 B1217 B1222 B1223

Sutton Howgrave
Kirklington
Sinderby
Ainderby Quernhow
Carlton Miniott
Sowerby
Bagby
Whitestonecliffe
Osgodby Hall
Great Thirkleby
Kilburn
Oldstead
Wass
Ampleforth
Skipton-on-Swale
Baldersby
Catton
Topcliffe Airfield
Little Thirkleby
Shandy Hall
Byland Abbey
Coxwold
Newburgh Priory
Thorpe Hall
Wath
Melmerby
Norton Conyers
Topcliffe
Dalton
Asenby
Sessay
Thormanby
Hutton Sessay
Husthwaite
Oulston
Yearsley
Rainton
Hutton Conyers
Sharow
Dishforth
Cundall
Crakehill
Raskelf
Crayke
Copt Hewick
Marton-le-Moor
Bridge Hewick
Littlethorpe
Newby Hall
Dishforth Airfield
Norton-le-Clay
Brafferton
Helperby
Easingwold
Tholthorpe
Alne
Cross Lanes
Huby
Skelton on Ure
Kirby Hill
Langthorpe
Myton-on-Swale
Flawith
Tollerton
Youlton
South Stainley
Bishop Monkton
Burton Leonard
Roecliffe
Minskip
Grafton
Lower Dunsforth
Upper Dunsforth
Aldwark
Toll
Linton-on-Ouse
Newton-on-Ouse
Brearton
Farnham
Arkendale
Marton
Great Ouseburn
Little Ouseburn
Thorpe Underwood
Nun Monkton
Shipton
Wigginton
Nidd
Scotton
Ferrensby
Coneythorpe
Flaxby
Whixley
Green Hammerton
Moor Monkton
Beningbrough
Skelton
Scriven
Goldsborough
Little Ribston
Cattal
Walshford
Hunsingore
Kirk Hammerton
Nether Poppleton
Upper Poppleton
Castle
Plumpton Rocks
North Deighton
Cowthorpe
Tockwith
Hessay
Knapton
Rufforth
Follifoot
Spofforth
Kirk Deighton
Bickerton
Hutton Wandesley
Askham Bryan
Kirkby Overblow
Stockeld Park
Bilton in Ainsty
Angram
Askham Richard
Bilbrough
Sicklinghall
Clap Gate
Linton
Walton
Trading Estate
Healaugh
Wighill
Catterton
Copmanthorpe
Netherby
Collingham
Boston Spa
Thorp Arch
Newton Kyme
Colton
Acaster Malbis
Harewood
East Keswick
Bardsey
Clifford
Appleton Roebuck
Arthington
Eccup
Holme Green
Bolton Percy
Acaster Selby
Scarcroft
Bramham
Stutton
Kirby Wharfe
Bramham Park
Kiddal Lane End
Ulleskelf
Ryther
Thorner
Shadwell
Barwick in Elmet
Aberford
Towton
Chapel Allerton
Roundhay
Scholes
Pendas Fields
Saxton
Church Fenton
Wistow
Headingley
Garforth
Old Micklefield
Mickletown
Micklefield
Sherburn
Little Fenton
Biggin
Beeston
Temple Newsam House
Swillington
Barkston Ash
Woodlesford
Oulton
Great Preston
Ledston
Fairburn
Hillam
Burton Salmon
Rothwell
Carlton
Methley
Allerton Bywater
New Fryston
Birkin
West Haddlesey
Middleton
Robin Hood
Mickletown
Brotherton
Beal
Kellington

River Swale
River Ure
River Nidd
River Wharfe
River Ouse
River Aire
Cock Beck
Selby Canal

DERE STREET
ROMAN ROAD
RIDGE

Marston Moor
Bramham Park
Eccup Reservoir

ISVRIVM

11
4
24
8
22
5

SCALE 1:250 000 or 1 INCH to 4 MILES 1CM to 2.5KM
KILOMETRES
MILES
0   2   4   6   8   10   15
0   2   4   6   8   10
KEYMAP HEIGHTS SHOWN IN FEET

Keymap 1

Sproxton
Harome
R Rye
Riccal
B1257
waldkirk
Nunnington
Hall
West Ness
Normanby
Little Barugh
Muscoates
West Ness
Salton
Kirby Misperton
7
A169
B1258
Gilling East
Stonegrave
Cawton
East Ness
Butterwick
Little Habton
Great Habton
Ryton
Low Marishes
West Knapton
East Knapton
B1363
Hovingham
Fryton
Slingsby
Barton-le-Street
Amotherby
Broughton
Wykeham
64
Old Malton
Scampston
15
A
Coulton
Scackleton
Appleton-le-Street
Swinton
B1257
Rillington 117
Thorpe Bassett
Wintring
Stearsby
Howardian Hills
Coneysthorpe
196
MALTON
Scagglethorpe
Place Newto
Skewsby
Terrington
Ganthorpe
Castle Howard
NORTON-ON-DERWENT
Settrington
654
Whenby
Farlington
Bulmer
Great Lake
High Hutton
Welburn
Huttons Ambo
North Grimston
Duggleby
Dugglel Howe
B1253
Sheriff Hutton
19
Whitwell-on-the-Hill
13
Kirkham Priory
Langton
Kennythorpe
Birdsall
Wharram le Street
B1248
West Lilling
Thornton-le-Clay
Foston
Crambe
7
Leavening
Burythorpe
Wharram Percy Village
Wolds Way
3
Burdale
Flaxton
18
Barton-le-Willows
Howsham
Harton
Bossall
755
Acklam
776
Thixendale
Fimber
A64
Claxton
Sand Hutton
Scrayingham
Leppington
807
Kirby Underdale
28
Fridaythorpe
Strensall
Towthorpe
Buttercrambe
Bugthorpe
793
17
Earswick
Skirpenbeck
ROMAN ROAD
Huggate
510
untington
Stockton on the Forest
Upper Helmsley
54
Stamford Bridge
19
Youllthorpe
Bishop Wilton
Great Givendale
New Earswick
Warthill
Gate Helmsley
1066
Full Sutton
Wolds Way
A1036
A166
Holtby
Low Catton
High Catton
Fangfoss
Meltonby
9
YORK
EBVRACVM
Murton
Dunnington
Bolton
Yapham
Millington
668
Warter
Heslington
A64
A1079
Wilberfoss
27
Pocklington
480
Fulford
B1228
Kexby
18
Barmby Moor
B1246
Newton upon Derwent
Nunburnholme
496
opthorpe
Elvington
54
Sutton upon Derwent
Allerthorpe
Hayton
Burnby
aburn
Crockey Hill
Thornton
ROMAN ROAD
Londesborough
Deighton
Pocklington Canal
Thorpe le Street
Shiptonthorpe
Wheldrake
Melbourne
Bielby
Everingham
Goodmanham
Escrick
13
Thorganby
East Cottingwith
Seaton Ross
Market Weighton
21
ngfleet
Skipwith
Ellerton
Laytham
A614
Wolds Way
North Duffield
Aughton
Harlthorpe
A163
Holme-on-Spalding-Moor
North Cliffe
Sancton
ROMAN ROAD
Riccall
17
Foggathorpe
Moor End
Sand Hole
South Cliffe
9
A1034
Nor
A19
Highfield
Bubwith
A614
13
South
Barlby
Osgodby
Lund
Gunby
Willitoft
Gribthorpe
Spaldington
Bursea
North Cave
Hotham
SELBY
Cliffe
South Duffield
Breighton
20
Wressle
B1228
Brind
Portington
Sandholme
North Cave
Everthorpe
West End
Hemingbrough
A63
Newsholme
A63
Ellerker
A1041
Barmby on the Marsh
Howden
12
Eastrington
Gilberdyke
Newport
Walling Fen
12
Barlow
Long Drax
Knedlington
Staddlethorpe
Broomfleet
Drax Power Station
Asselby
M62
Balkholme
B1230
Temple Hirst
Drax
Kilpin
37
Skelton
Laxton
Camblesforth

Keymap 2

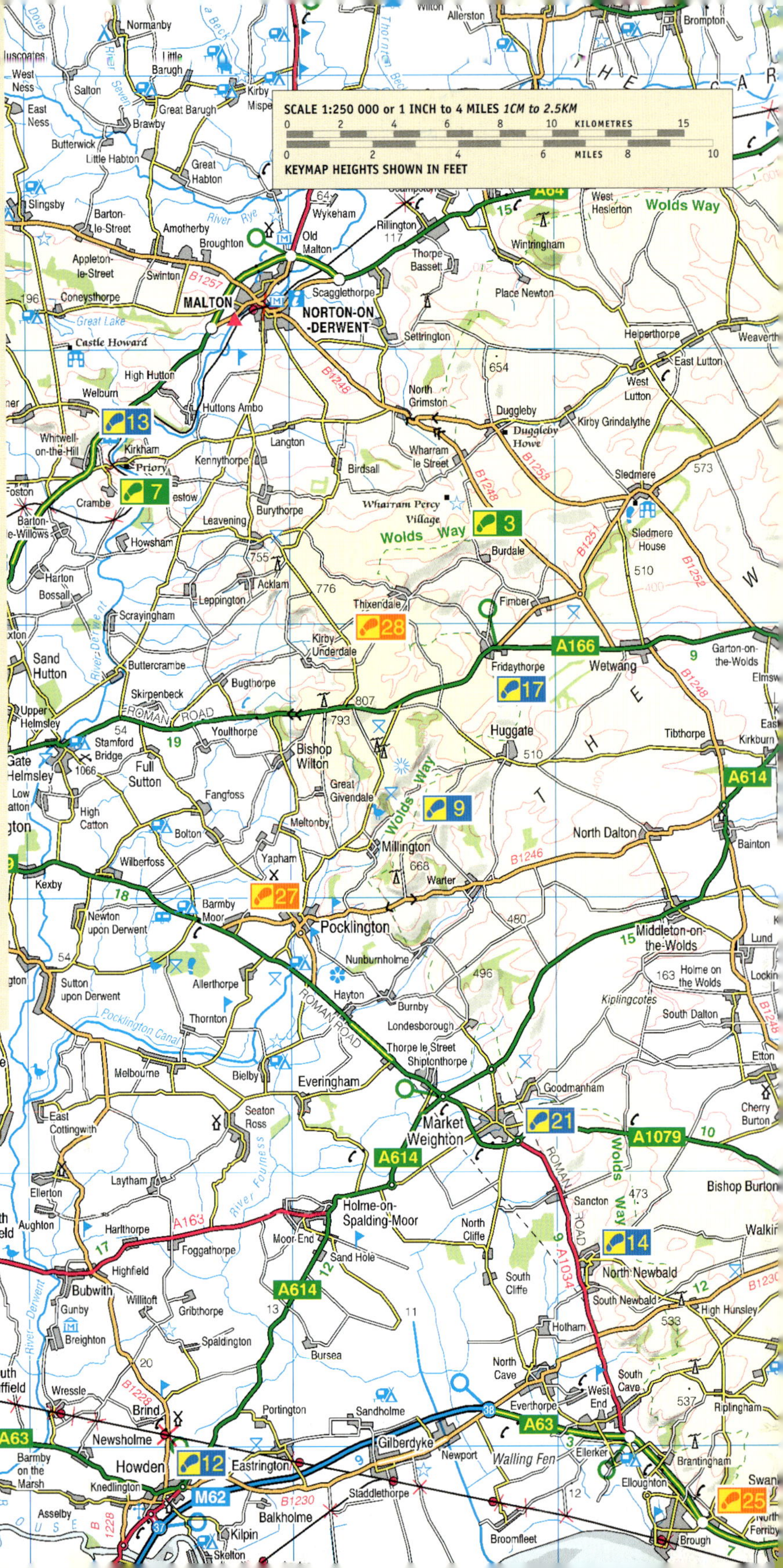

SCALE 1:250 000 or 1 INCH to 4 MILES 1CM to 2.5KM
0 2 4 6 8 10 KILOMETRES 15
0 2 4 6 8 10 MILES
KEYMAP HEIGHTS SHOWN IN FEET

Normanby
Wilton
Allerston
Brompton
Luscoates
West Ness
Salton
Little Barugh
Kirby Misperton
East Ness
Butterwick
Brawby
Great Barugh
Little Habton
Great Habton
THE CAR
Slingsby
Barton-le-Street
Amotherby
Broughton
River Rye
Wykeham
64
Old Malton
Rillington
117
Thorpe Bassett
Wintringham
Scampston
A64
15
West Hesterton
Wolds Way
Appleton-le-Street
Swinton
B1257
Coneysthorpe
196
MALTON
Scagglethorpe
NORTON-ON-DERWENT
Settrington
Place Newton
Helperthorpe
Weaverth
Great Lake
Castle Howard
Welburn
High Hutton
Huttons Ambo
B1248
North Grimston
654
Duggleby
Duggleby Howe
Kirby Grindalythe
West Lutton
East Lutton
13
Whitwell-on-the-Hill
Kirkham Priory
Kennythorpe
Langton
Birdsall
Wharram le Street
B1253
Sledmere
573
Foston
7
estow
Leavening
Burythorpe
Wharram Percy Village
Wolds Way
3
Burdale
B1248
B1251
Sledmere House
510
B1252
Crambe
Barton-le-Willows
Howsham
755
Acklam
776
Thixendale
28
Fimber
9
Garton-on-the-Wolds
Elmsw
Harton
Bossall
Leppington
Scrayingham
Kirby Underdale
Wolds Way
A166
Wetwang
B1248
East Kirkburn
Sand Hutton
Buttercrambe
Bugthorpe
807
Fridaythorpe
17
THE
xton
Upper Helmsley
ROMAN ROAD
Youlthorpe
793
Huggate
510
Tibthorpe
Gate Helmsley
Stamford Bridge
54
19
Bishop Wilton
Full Sutton
Fangfoss
Great Givendale
Wolds Way
9
North Dalton
A614
Bainton
Low atton
1066
High Catton
Bolton
Meltonby
Millington
B1246
Wilberfoss
Yapham
668
Warter
Kexby
18
Barmby Moor
27
Pocklington
480
Middleton-on-the-Wolds
15
Lund
Lockin
ngton
Newton upon Derwent
Nunburnholme
496
163
Holme on the Wolds
B124B
Sutton upon Derwent
54
Allerthorpe
Hayton
Burnby
Kiplingcotes
South Dalton
Pocklington Canal
Thornton
Londesborough
Etton
Wheldrake
Melbourne
Bielby
Thorpe le Street
Shiptonthorpe
Everingham
Goodmanham
Cherry Burton
Thorganby
East Cottingwith
Seaton Ross
Market Weighton
21
A1079
10
Bishop Burton
North Duffield
Ellerton
Aughton
Laytham
Harlthorpe
A163
River Foulness
17
Holme-on-Spalding-Moor
Moor End
A614
North Cliffe
Sancton
473
ROMAN ROAD
14
Walki
Highfield
Foggathorpe
Sand Hole
12
9
A1034
North Newbald
Bubwith
Willitoft
Gribthorpe
A614
13
South Cliffe
South Newbald
High Hunsley
12
B1230
Gunby
Breighton
Spaldington
11
Hotham
533
South Duffield
Wressle
Brind
20
Bursea
Portington
Sandholme
North Cave
West End
South Cave
537
Riplingham
Cliffe
A63
Newsholme
B1228
Howden
12
Eastrington
Gilberdyke
Newport
Walling Fen
A63
Everthorpe
Ellerker
3
Brantingham
25
Barmby on the Marsh
Knedlington
M62
Kilpin
B1230
Staddlethorpe
9
Elloughton
Brough
Swan
Drax
Asselby
Balkholme
Broomfleet
Skelton

Keymap 2

Lebberston
Gristhorpe
FILEY
Filey Bay
10
River Hertford
Flixton
Willerby
Folkton
A1039
Muston
Staxton
Ganton
Wolds Way
Hunmanby
20
Reighton Sands
Holiday Village
Reighton
Fordon
Speeton
Crab Rocks
Wold Newton
Burton Fleming
Grindale
Bempton
Danes' Dyke
Holiday Centre
FLAMBOROUGH HEAD
Foxholes
Willy Howe
A165
Flamborough
1
15
Butterwick
Thwing
Sewerby
Langtoft
Boynton
B1253
Rudston
BRIDLINGTON
A614
Hilderthorpe
Kilham
ROMAN ROAD
Haisthorpe
Thornholme
Carnaby
A165
BRIDLINGTON BAY
Langtoft
365
Hall
79
Burton Agnes
Fraisthorpe
Ruston Parva
Harpham
18
Lowthorpe
Gransmoor
A614
Nafferton
Great Kelk
Barmston
DRIFFIELD
Wansford
Lissett
Ulrome
ttle Driffield
Kelk Beck
Gembling
B1242
eythorpe
Foston on the Wolds
Old Howe
B1249
Skerne
Beeford
Dringhoe Castle
Skipsea
Brigham
North Frodingham
Skipsea Brough
Hutton Cranswick
16
Dunnington
Rotsea
Hempholme
Bewholme
Atwick
Watton
16
Burshill
23
HORNSEA
Beswick
Brandesburton
Hornsea Mere
River Hull
Seaton
Canal
Leven
B1244
Sigglesthorne
Goxhill
Rolston
Scorborough
Catwick
Aike
Arram
Routh
Little Hatfield
Mappleton
Leconfield
Rise
Great Hatfield
A1035
Long Riston
26
Tickton
A165
Great Cowden
BEVERLEY
Withernwick
Molescroft
Weel
Meaux
New Ellerby
Skirlaugh
West Newton
Aldbrough
Woodmansey
Wawne
Old Ellerby
A164
A1079
Thearne
Bransholme
Dunswell
Swine
Burton Constable Hall
Bentley
COTTINGHAM
Ganstead
Coniston
Flinton
Garton
A1079
Sutton-on-Hull
Bilton
Sproatley
Humbleton
Grimston
Fitling
Owstwick
Willerby
B1233
Lelley
A165
Marfleet
Preston
Elstronwick
Roos
Kirk Ella
2
KINGSTON UPON HULL
HEDON
Anlaby
Burstwick
B1362
Rimswell
6
Toll
A63
Paull
Thorngumbald
Halsham

Walk	Page	Start	Nat. Grid Reference	Distance	Time	Highest Point
Beverley	79	Beverley, Market Cross	TA 034397	9 miles (14.5km)	4½ hrs	154ft (47m)
Boroughbridge and Aldborough	20	Boroughbridge	SE 396666	4½ miles (7.2km)	2 hrs	82ft (25m)
Danes Dyke and Sewerby	14	Danes Dyke car park off B1255	TA 215696	2½ miles (4km)	1½ hrs	114ft (35m)
Flamborough Head	44	Flamborough Head, South Landing	TA 231697	7 miles (11.3km)	3½ hrs	147ft (45m)
Fridaythorpe and Huggate	50	Fridaythorpe	SE 875593	6½ miles (10.5km)	3 hrs	689ft (210m)
Harpham, Burton Agnes and Kilham	53	Bracey Bridge picnic site	TA 077619	7 miles (11.3km)	3½ hrs	200ft (61m)
Hedon	16	Hedon	TA 188286	4 miles (6.4km)	2 hrs	13ft (4m)
Hornsea Mere and the Rail Trail	69	Hornsea, Marine Drive and New Road	TA 208479	8½ miles (13.7km)	4 hrs	67ft (20m)
Howden Marsh and the River Ouse	38	Howden	SE 748283	6½ miles (10.5km)	3 hrs	18ft (5m)
Humber Estuary	24	Humber Bridge Country Park	TA 021259	5½ miles (8.9km)	2½ hrs	96ft (30m)
Hunmanby, Muston and Stocking Dale	59	Hunmanby	TA 096775	7½ miles (12.1km)	3½ hrs	418ft (127m)
Kirkham Priory and the River Derwent	26	Kirkham	SE 738658	5 miles (8km)	2½ hrs	262ft (80m)
Londesborough Park and Goodmanham	62	Market Weighton	SE 877417	7½ miles (12.1km)	3½ hrs	279ft (85m)
Lotherton Hall and Aberford	22	Lotherton Hall	SE 448362	5 miles (8km)	2½ hrs	246ft (75m)
Millington Dale	30	Millington Wood	SE 838530	5 miles (8km)	2½ hrs	609ft (185m)
Nether Poppleton and the River Ouse	73	Nether Poppleton	SE 560549	9 miles (14.5km)	4½ hrs	52ft (16m)
Newbald Wold	42	North Newbald	SE 913367	5½ miles (8.9km)	3 hrs	475ft (144m)
North Cliff and Filey Brigg	32	Filey, The Crescent/ N. Cliff Country Park	TA 117805	5 miles (8km)	2½ hrs	226ft (69m)
Pocklington Canal and Allerthorpe Common	83	Pocklington	SE 804489	9½ miles (15.3km)	4½ hrs	96ft (30m)
Ripon and the rivers Skell and Ure	35	Ripon, Market Place	SE 310713	5½ miles (8.9km)	2½ hrs	82ft (25m)
Sheriff Hutton and Mowthorpe Hill	56	Sheriff Hutton	SE 651664	7 miles (11.3km)	3½ hrs	355ft (108m)
Tadcaster and Healaugh	66	Tadcaster	SE 488435	8 miles (12.9km)	4 hrs	72ft (22m)
Thixendale and Kirby Underdale	87	Thixendale	SE 843612	8 miles (12.9km)	4 hrs	751ft (229m)
Tockwith and the River Nidd	28	Tockwith	SE 468524	5½ miles (8.9km)	2½ hrs	56ft (17m)
Watton and Kilnwick	47	Watton Green	TA 018500	7 miles (11.3km)	3½ hrs	114ft (35m)
Welburn and Castle Howard	40	Welburn post office	SE 711679	5½ miles (8.9km)	2½ hrs	229ft (70m)
Welton Dale and Brantingham Wold	76	Welton	SE 958276	8½ miles (13.7km)	4 hrs	459ft (140m)
Wharram Percy	18	Wharram Percy	SE 867645	2½ miles (4km)	1½ hrs	685ft (209m)

Comments

This walk takes you across the pleasant countryside to the south of Beverley. Near the end, there are superb views over the town, minster and the flat lands beyond.

An attractive stretch beside the River Ure is followed by a visit to the site of a Roman town. A brief detour enables you to see three prehistoric monoliths.

There is plenty of interest on this short and easy walk: superb coastal views, a wooded ravine, a prehistoric earthwork and an 18th-century hall.

This is a walk of fine seascapes and dramatic cliff scenery as you follow a winding clifftop path around the chalk headland of Flamborough Head.

The walk takes you through a typical wolds landscape of sweeping uplands and deep, dry valleys, and there are extensive views.

This walk links three attractive villages near the foot of the wolds and passes a fine Elizabethan mansion.

There are wide views across the flat landscape of Holderness on this walk around the town of Hedon.

On the opening stretch you pass by Hornsea Mere, and the return leg makes use of a disused railway track. There are wide views across Holderness.

A short stroll through Howden Marsh is followed by a much longer walk along embankments above the River Ouse.

An invigorating walk beside the Humber Estuary, which is inevitably dominated by the soaring elegance of the Humber Bridge.

The route passes through two attractive villages, and the highlight is a walk through a beautiful wooded dale.

A pleasant walk through woodland and across fields is followed by a beautiful ramble beside the River Derwent. There are fine views of the ruins of Kirkham Priory.

This fine walk in the wolds includes a market town, two villages, medieval churches, parkland and extensive views across the Vale of York.

This varied walk starts by a large Edwardian house and includes parkland, woodland and the village of Aberford.

Millington is a delightful village, and there are dramatic views over Millington Dale and a lovely finale through Millington Wood to a fine viewpoint.

A walk across fields to the confluence of the rivers Nidd and Ouse is followed by a lengthy and attractive ramble beside the Ouse.

From the village of North Newbald gentle slopes lead up over the wolds, and there are fine views throughout.

The route includes fine cliff walking, the dramatic headland of Filey Brigg and sweeping views across Filey Bay to Flamborough Head.

There are fine views across the Vale of York and the western edge of the wolds, attractive walking by the Pocklington Canal and some lovely woodland towards the end.

There is some delightful riverside walking beside the rivers Skell and Ure in the vicinity of the cathedral city of Ripon.

Starting near the church and castle ruins at Sheriff Hutton, this walk in the Howardian Hills gives you fine views over the Vale of York to the line of the wolds.

The walk takes you across the gently undulating country of the Wharfe valley to the north of Tadcaster.

This is high wolds country at its finest, with two small but attractive villages, extensive views and a real feeling of remoteness.

There is pleasant walking beside the River Nidd, and the wide views across the Vale of York include the Civil War battlefield of Marston Moor.

This is a flat walk near the foot of the wolds. Both Watton and Kilnwick have interesting old churches, and near the end you pass the site of a medieval priory.

Most of the walk is through the grounds of the Castle Howard estate, and there are fine views of the great house and some of the other buildings in the park.

A combination of wooded valleys, open hillsides, grand views and two picturesque villages – both with superb churches – creates a most enjoyable and satisfying walk.

England's most complete deserted medieval village site and its ruined church are the focal points of this fine wolds walk.

Introduction to the Vale of York and Yorkshire Wolds

Yorkshire is a great area for walking, and it is not surprising that England's largest county contains a wide variety of terrain. For obvious reasons walkers tend to flock to the two national parks, Yorkshire Dales and North York Moors, and to the 'Brontë country' of the South Pennines, but this huge county has much more to offer.

The wide plain of the Vale of York is the very heart of the county, watered by its principal rivers and containing the great city of York. Travelling eastwards across the vale, the western escarpment of the Yorkshire Wolds can be seen on the horizon. These rolling uplands exhibit all the characteristics of chalk country and are the most northerly chalk area in Britain, ending at the dramatic cliffs of Flamborough Head. Unlike other parts of Yorkshire, both the vale and wolds are mainly given over to arable farming, and their gentle landscapes are reminiscent of parts of southern England, a comment one could never make about the sterner terrain of either the Pennines or the North York Moors.

Vale of York

The Vale of York is a large area of predominantly flat country bordered by the Pennines in the west, the Howardian Hills and beyond them the North York Moors in the north east, and the Yorkshire Wolds in the east. To the south, the vale merges into the flat lands that extend beyond the River Ouse into Lincolnshire and South Yorkshire.

The main rivers through the Vale of York come from the Pennines to the west, flowing down through the Yorkshire Dales and on to the Humber. The Swale, Ure and Nidd join to form the Ouse, which then continues through York. South of the city, the river is enlarged by the Wharfe, Aire and Don and also the Derwent, the latter the only tributary the Ouse receives from the eastern rather than the western moorlands. After the Trent joins the Ouse, beyond

The Vale of York near Tockwith

Goole, the combined rivers become the mighty Humber Estuary and continue on to the North Sea. Most of these rivers are featured in the selection of walks in this guide, and their embankments provide generally easy and trouble-free walking, as well as giving extensive views across the vale.

At the heart of the vale stands the historic city of York, traditional capital of the North of England. Originally

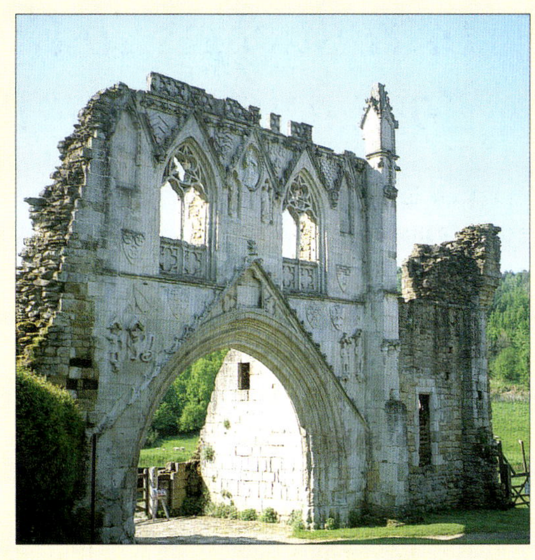

The gatehouse of Kirkham Priory

founded by the Romans as Eboracum, it became the capital, both political and ecclesiastical, of the Anglo-Saxon kingdom of Northumbria and, for a time, the centre of a Viking kingdom. Its great minster, seat of the archbishops of York, is the largest medieval church in England and one of the largest in Europe. The city flourished throughout the Middle Ages and later – it was an important inland port – and only when the Industrial Revolution spawned the giant new cities of Leeds, Bradford and Sheffield did York lose its dominant position. However, it still remains, in spirit if not in size, the capital of the North. Apart from the minster, there are a vast number of attractions in the city.

On the northern edge of the Vale of York, the Howardian Hills – an Area of Outstanding Natural Beauty – act as a sort of buffer between the vale and North York Moors. They offer fine walking, and from their slopes many views encompass both the vale and the wolds.

Yorkshire Wolds

To the east lie the wolds, the northern limits of a continuous band of chalk uplands that extends across the country in a north-easterly direction. From Dorset this band first heads across Salisbury Plain, through the Oxfordshire and Berkshire Downs and on to the Chilterns and the gentle heights of East Anglia. To the north of the Wash, it becomes the Lincolnshire Wolds and finally reappears on the other side of the Humber as the Yorkshire Wolds. The wolds end at Flamborough Head, between Bridlington and Filey.

This is classic chalk country at its finest, a landscape of rolling hills and deep, dry valleys punctuated by small areas of woodland, farms and scattered villages. It is sparsely populated country, and in some of the tiny

Kilham

and remote villages, tucked away in almost secretive valleys, the 21st century hardly seems to have intruded, which is very much part of their appeal. The large number of place names ending in either -by or -thorpe are an indication of Viking influence in this area and proof of probable large-scale Viking settlement.

York and Beverley are the obvious gateways into the area but the wolds are also ringed by a series of small market towns – Malton, Pocklington, Market Weighton and Driffield – as well as the coastal resorts of Bridlington and Filey.

Compared with the other upland areas of Yorkshire, the wolds are intensively farmed and overwhelmingly arable, although there is some sheep farming. Walking is excellent and, although the slopes are generally gentle, the wolds do rise to more than 800ft (244m) and can provide reasonably challenging routes for the more energetic and adventurous walkers. The walks often follow clear and broad tracks from which there are seemingly endless views across deep valleys and rolling hills. The views from the western escarpment are particularly impressive, looking across the Vale of York.

Holderness

Lying between the wolds, North Sea and Humber Estuary is the roughly triangular-shaped, flat coastal region of Holderness, an area of rich sheep pastures. In the Middle Ages this was a wealthy area, as can be seen from the number of exceptionally large and fine churches that preside over what are now quite small places. Particularly impressive are the churches at Hedon and Patrington, known respectively as the 'king and queen of Holderness'. The finest churches of all are to be found in the delightful and historic town of Beverley, whose skyline is filled not only by the towers of its magnificent minster but also by the almost equally impressive St Mary's Church.

Much of the wealth of these towns came from river trade but in time the many small ports along the Humber and its tributaries – both on the

Yorkshire and Lincolnshire banks of the river – were eclipsed by Edward I's new town of Kingston (King's Town), built at the confluence of the Humber and Hull. Here is to be found the largest parish church in the whole of England, and over the centuries Hull developed into one of the world's greatest fishing ports.

The flat coast of Holderness has a number of sandy beaches, and in Victorian times rail links with Hull and the other large cities of Yorkshire led to the development of small seaside resorts at Withernsea and Hornsea. The major resorts were farther north, at Bridlington and Filey, both of which lie on wide sandy bays with superb cliffs.

Although there are no hills in Holderness, the combination of huge skies and open expanses – reminiscent of the Cambridgeshire Fens in some ways – has its attractions so some walks have been included in this relatively little-known area.

Walking in the area

The Wolds Way is the major long-distance route. Starting on the Humber Estuary, within sight of the great bridge, it heads across the wolds to finish at Filey Brigg. Its northern end coincides with the southern end of the Cleveland Way, and the two paths together provide continuously fine walking across a large slice of Yorkshire, from the Humber to Helmsley.

Other long-distance routes include the Minster Way – between York and Beverley – and the Centenary Way. Some disused railway lines have been converted into footpaths and cycleways. These include the Hudson Way, between Beverley and Market Weighton, and the Hornsea Trail, between Hull and Hornsea.

One advantage of walking on this eastern side of England is that it has a drier climate, although the wolds in particular can get heavy snowfalls in winter. Calm days at any time of year can result in the notorious sea-frets (mists) on the North Sea coast but on such days a few miles journey inland may reward you with sunshine, blue skies and clear conditions.

First-time visitors to this area may well be agreeably surprised by its variety of terrain and excellent walking facilities, whether it be flat and easy strolls beside the rivers of the Vale of York, the dramatic coastal walks near Flamborough Head or the more energetic rambles over the open hillsides and through the steep-sided dales of the chalk wolds.

Brantingham Dale

Danes Dyke and Sewerby

Start	Danes Dyke car park, off B1255 between Bridlington and Flamborough
Distance	2½ miles (4km)
Approximate time	1½ hours
Parking	Danes Dyke
Refreshments	Pubs and cafés at Sewerby, café at Sewerby Hall
Ordnance Survey maps	Landranger 101 (Scarborough), Explorers 295 (Bridlington, Driffield & Hornsea) or 301 (Scarborough, Bridlington & Flamborough Head),

Although a short walk, there is much of interest. It starts at a dramatic wooded ravine and passes an 18th-century country house with fine gardens. The extensive views take in the nearby resort of Bridlington, with its superb sandy beaches, and the chalk cliffs of Flamborough Head.

Danes Dyke, on the eastern side of the thickly wooded ravine, is a linear earthwork, about 2½ miles (4km) long, which stretches across the neck of the Flamborough peninsula. Despite its name, it is thought to have been constructed during the Iron Age rather than by the Vikings.

🐾 Leave the car park and, at a public bridleway sign, turn left

Flamborough Head from Sewerby

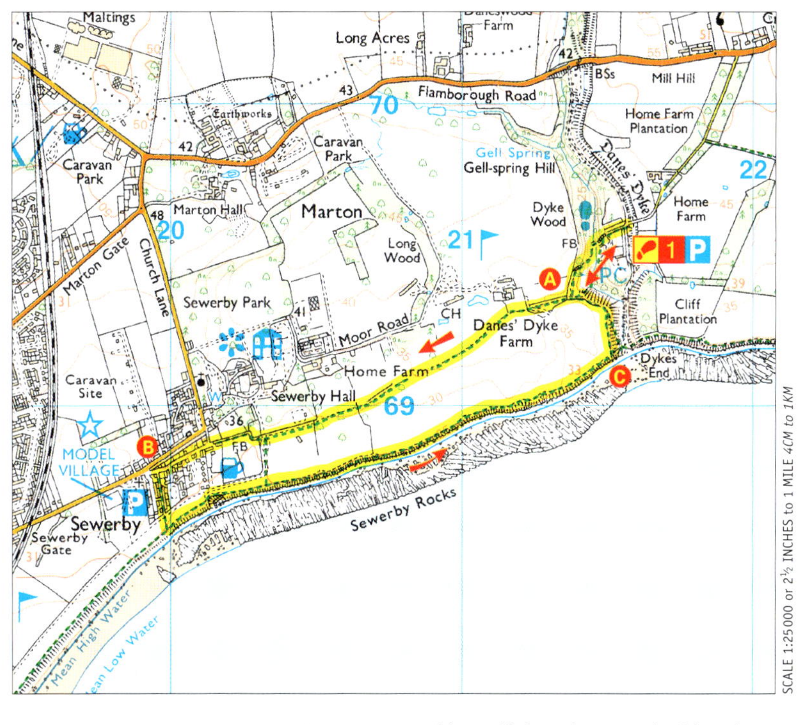

alongside a wall on the left. Descend
gently through the beautiful woodland
of the ravine and go down steps to
reach the bottom. Turn right to cross a
footbridge over a stream, turn left and,
at a fork, take the right-hand path.
Climb more steps, bear left to continue
along the right, inside edge of the trees
and descend steps to a T-junction **(A)**.

Turn right along a path that heads in
a fairly straight line – initially by a
hedge on the right, before it becomes
enclosed and later continues across a
golf course. After passing through a belt
of trees, head across fields and continue
along the right-hand edge of a cricket
ground, passing in front of Sewerby
Hall. This elegant Georgian mansion,
originally built by John Greame
between 1714 and 1720, was extended
later in the 18th century and then again
during the Victorian period. The house
is situated amidst very fine parkland

and beautiful gardens overlooking the
North Sea.

After passing the entrance to the hall
and gardens, keep ahead along an
enclosed tarmac path, which bends first
right and then left to emerge onto a
road in Sewerby village by the Ship Inn.
Keep ahead and, at a public footpath
sign to Cliff Top, turn left along an
enclosed path **(B)**. Cross a tarmac track
and, as you head across grass to the
edge of the cliffs, there are superb views
on both sides – Bridlington and its
harbour to the right and Flamborough
Head to the left.

Turn left onto a tarmac path and,
where this ends, keep ahead along the
grassy cliff top as far as the Danes Dyke
ravine **(C)**. The path turns left, away
from the sea along the top of the ravine,
and then bears right to a T-junction.
Turn left along the left-hand inside
edge of the woodland to the next
T-junction **(A)** and turn right. Here you
rejoin the outward route and retrace
your steps to the start.

Hedon

Start	Hedon
Distance	4 miles (6.4km)
Approximate time	2 hours
Parking	Hedon
Refreshments	Pubs and café at Hedon
Ordnance Survey maps	Landranger 107 (Kingston upon Hull), Explorers 292 (Withernsea & Spurn Head) and 293 (Kingston upon Hull & Beverley)

The walk is basically a circuit around the town of Hedon, making use of tracks, paths and a disused railway line. Almost half the route is beside Burstwick Drain, and there are extensive vistas across the flat landscape of Holderness as well as closer views of the tower of Hedon's imposing church.

Hedon was founded around 1130 and by the 13th century was a flourishing port and market town on the Humber Estuary. Silting up in Hedon Haven, which linked the port with the river, and the rise of nearby Hull led to its subsequent decline. Its former prosperity, however, is reflected in its magnificent church, of cathedral-like dimensions and appearance, nicknamed the 'King of Holderness'. It was mostly

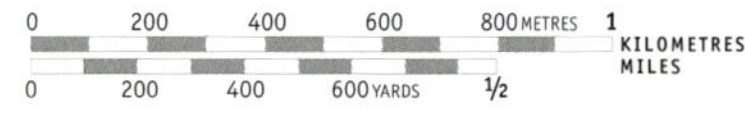

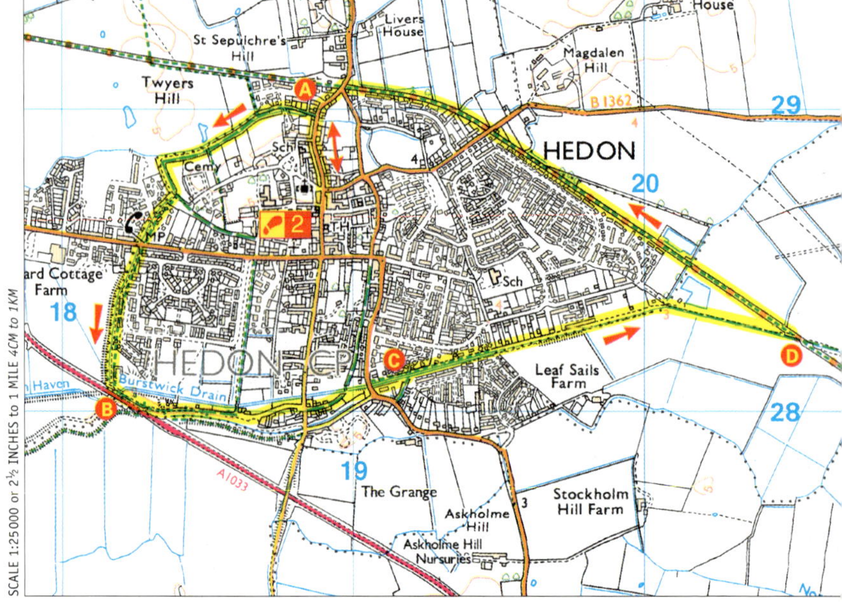

built in the 13th and 14th centuries and is dominated by its superb Perpendicular central tower, 129ft (39m) high.

The walk starts in the Market Place. Facing the post office and church, turn right along Soutter Gate and, at a public bridleway sign, turn left **A** along a track (Twyers Lane). Cross a road and keep ahead along an attractive, tree-lined track above drains both sides. Across the flat fields to the right, Preston church tower can be seen. On reaching a kissing-gate, do not go through but turn left to continue along the tree-lined track. Cross a footbridge over a drain and, at a fingerpost, turn right along a path that keeps by the drain on the right.

Cross a road, keep ahead to cross a main road and continue alongside the drain to a T-junction in front of Burstwick Drain. Turn right to cross it,

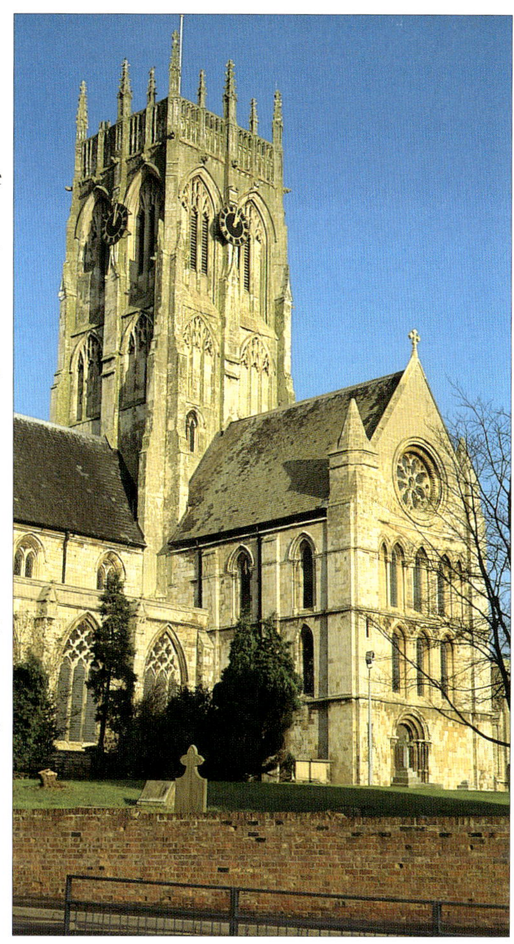

The magnificent Hedon church – the 'King of Holderness'

almost immediately turn sharp left **B**, cross a footbridge over another drain and keep ahead along a track, initially parallel to a road on the right. Bear left on joining another track, pass in front of the Haven Arms and continue along a lane to a T-junction. At a public bridleway sign, keep ahead along a tree-lined path to a footbridge over the drain. Do not cross it; continue ahead to pass beside a fence onto a road.

Cross over, take the path ahead along the right-hand bank of the drain to a T-junction and turn left to cross a footbridge. Turn right **C** onto an enclosed path, and the route continues along the left-hand bank of Burstwick Drain for the next $1/2$ mile (800m), eventually turning right to join a track. Where the track ends, by a bungalow, keep ahead along the right-hand edge of a field – still by the drain – to a T-junction to the left of a brick bridge and turn sharp left onto a straight, hedge-lined path **D**.

This is a disused railway track – part of the former Hull to Withernsea line – and you follow it back to Hedon. Cross one road, keep ahead to the next one and turn left. At a fork, take the right-hand road, which leads back to the starting point of the walk. ●

Wharram Percy

Start	Wharram Percy car park, signposted from B1248 between Wharram le Street and Wetwang
Distance	2½ miles (4km)
Approximate time	1½ hours
Parking	Wharram Percy
Refreshments	None
Ordnance Survey maps	Landranger 100 (Malton & Pickering), Explorer 300 (Howardian Hills & Malton)

The site of the deserted medieval village of Wharram Percy, the finest example of its kind in the country, occupies the slopes above Deep Dale and is the focal point of this short but highly scenic wolds walk. Particularly memorable is the stretch along the side of the dale, with views ahead of the ruined church, the most visible surviving relic of the largely vanished settlement.

Turn right out of the car park along the lane, follow it around a right-hand curve and, where it bends left **A**, keep ahead through a gate. Walk along a track, which initially passes along the left-hand edge of woodland and then continues along the left edge of fields.

After climbing a stile in the corner of the last field, turn right **B** – here

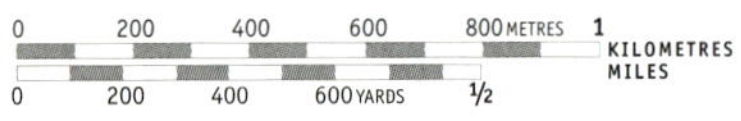

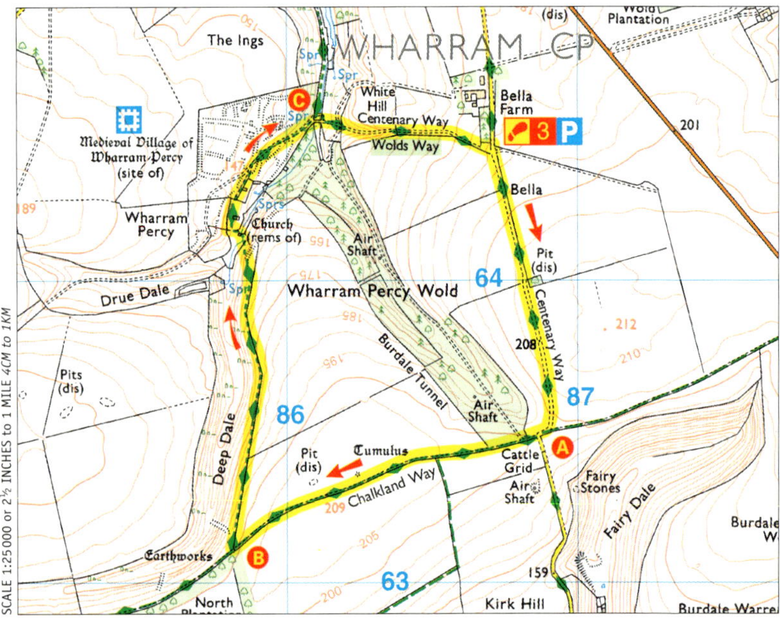

joining the Wolds Way – and walk along a grassy ledge above the steep-sided Deep Dale. Ahead the ruined church at Wharram Percy can be seen. Just beyond a footpath post, the path bears left and slants downhill across the slopes to a kissing-gate. Go through, keep ahead, passing to the right of a pond – a source of fish for the medieval villagers – and go through another kissing-gate into the churchyard.

Like many similar sites scattered throughout England, Wharram Percy became deserted in the later Middle Ages through a combination of the Black Death and a change from arable to mainly sheep farming. Although – apart from the church – there is little to see except mounds and earthworks, this is the best and most complete deserted village site in the country, and there is a series of information boards to enable you to identify the foundations of the peasant cottages, manor house, vicarage and other buildings. The medieval church continued in use until as late as 1949 because it served other villages in the locality and it became ruined after the tower collapsed in the 1950s.

Pass to the left of the church, go through a fence gap and keep ahead, passing the site of the medieval vicarage, to a kissing-gate by the corner of a brick building. Go through, keep ahead through the deserted village and bear right on joining another path. The path descends gently to a kissing-gate. Go through, descend steps and cross a footbridge over a brook **C**.

Climb steps, go through a kissing-gate and keep ahead to go through another one. Head uphill, going through one more kissing-gate, to return to the car park.

Wharram Percy

Boroughbridge and Aldborough

Start	Boroughbridge
Distance	4½ miles (7.2km). Shorter version 3½ miles (5.6km)
Approximate time	2 hours (1½ hours for short walk)
Parking	Boroughbridge
Refreshments	Pubs and cafés at Boroughbridge, pub at Aldborough
Ordnance Survey maps	Landranger 99 (Northallerton & Ripon), Explorer 299 (Ripon & Boroughbridge)

Not much more than ¹⁄₂ mile (800m) separates Boroughbridge and Aldborough but the first part of the walk takes a longer route beside the meandering River Ure. The more direct return is along a lane. A brief detour at the start enables you to see the Devil's Arrows, three prehistoric stones, and at Aldborough you can visit the site of a Roman town and a museum. There are wide views across the Vale of York to the line of the Hambleton Hills.

The pleasant town of Boroughbridge grew up as a crossing point over the River Ure on the Great North Road. It used to be busy with traffic but now it is bypassed and much quieter. The church was mainly rebuilt in the 19th century but retains a Norman doorway.

The walk begins by the ornate fountain in St James Square. *If doing the shorter route, take the road signposted to York (Aldborough Road).* For the initial short detour to the Devil's Arrows, walk along St Helena to a T-junction, turn left and turn right along Roecliffe Lane **A**. The Devil's Arrows comprise three great standing stones of millstone grit – there were originally four – thought to date from around 2700BC and brought here from the Knaresborough area, around 10 miles (16km) away.

Retrace your steps to St James Square and walk along Aldborough Road.

Where the main road bends right, keep ahead along a minor road and, at a public footpath sign, turn left through a kissing-gate **B** and walk along an enclosed path. After going through a gate, turn right and continue along an embankment above the River Ure **C**. There are several stiles as you follow the river around a sharp right-hand bend to eventually reach a T-junction **D**.

Turn right along an enclosed track to a lane and turn right into Aldborough. At a fork in front of a green, take the right-hand road for a direct return to the start but for the remains of the Roman town and museum take the left-hand road. At the next fork, take the left-hand road again, passing along the left side of a large green with a maypole, head uphill and follow the road around a right-hand bend to a T-junction **E**. The Roman museum and site of the town of Isurium Brigantium

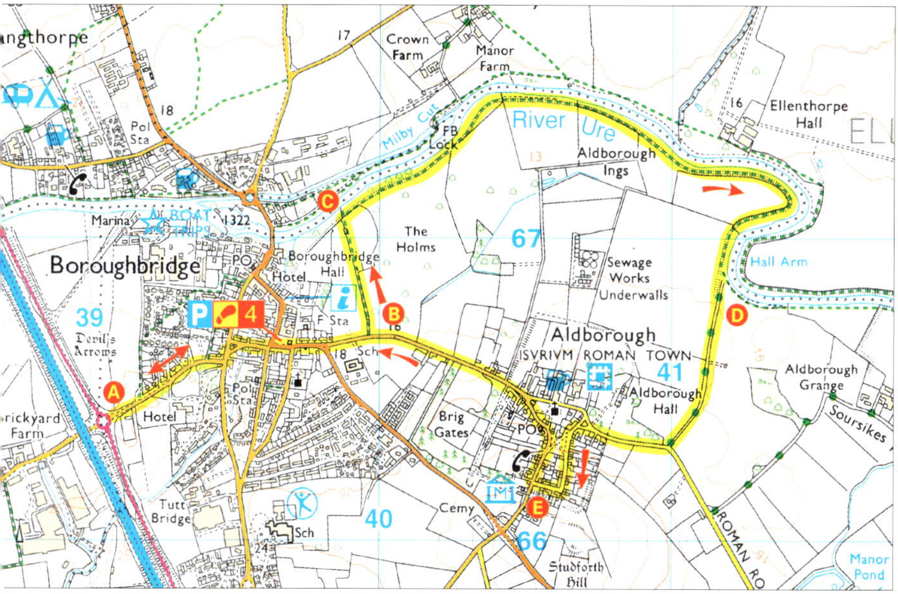

SCALE 1:25 000 or 2½ INCHES to 1 MILE *4CM to 1KM*

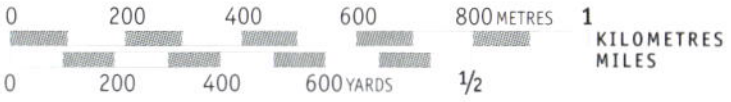

is just to the left. This was the principal town of the Brigantes tribe but now only fragments of the walls remain, although there are two fine mosaic pavements.

At the T-junction, turn right downhill into the village centre and keep to the left of the green with the maypole. The road curves left, passing to the left of the mainly 14th-century church, to a junction by another small green. Bear left and follow the quiet, tree-lined road back to Boroughbridge.

The River Ure near Boroughbridge

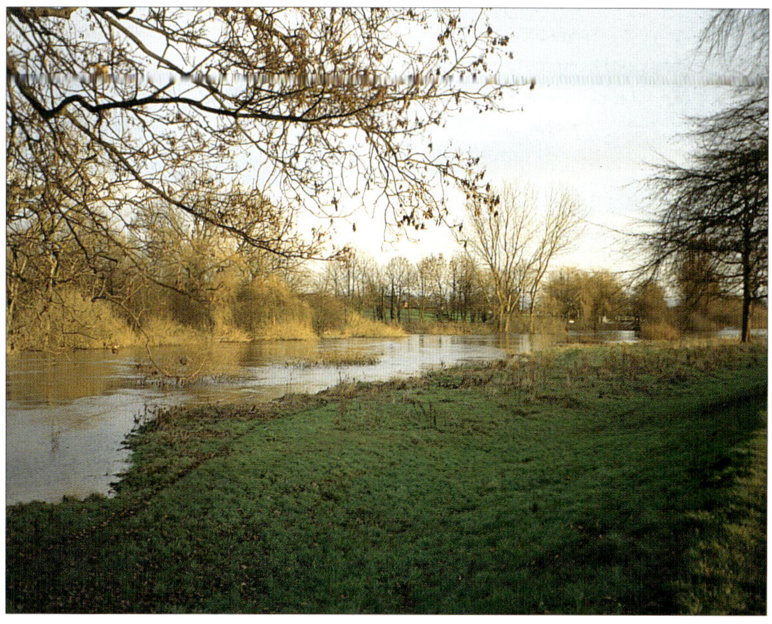

Lotherton Hall and Aberford

Start	Lotherton Hall, off minor road between Aberford and Towton about 1 mile (1.6km) east of Aberford
Distance	5 miles (8km)
Approximate time	2½ hours
Parking	Lotherton Hall
Refreshments	Café at Lotherton Hall, pubs at Aberford
Ordnance Survey maps	Landranger 105 (York & Selby), Explorer 289 (Leeds)

There is very much a Victorian flavour to this mainly flat, easy-paced and well-waymarked walk. The attractive gardens and parkland surrounding 19th-century Lotherton Hall make a fine start and finish. There are wide views across the Vale of York and, at about the half-way point, the route passes through the village of Aberford, with its imposing Victorian almshouses and church.

The grand Victorian mansion of Lotherton Hall belonged to the Gascoignes, a local colliery-owning family, and assumed its present form after a programme of enlargement and remodelling that began in 1893. Since 1968 it has been owned by the City of Leeds and houses a fine collection of paintings and furniture. Next to the hall is a tiny, plain Norman chapel and around it there are attractive gardens and a deer park.

Start by facing the stable block, turn left along a tarmac track and, at a crossroads, turn right, in the 'Formal Gardens and Estate Walks' direction. Pass to the right of the hall and chapel and, at a meeting of tracks and paths, keep ahead along a paved path to a gate. Go through, keep ahead along a stony track and, where it bends left to a gate, continue across the grass to a waymarked kissing-gate in the field corner.

Pass through the gate, walk along the left-hand edge of a field, continue between fields towards woodland and then keep along the right-hand edge of the trees to go through a gate into the wood. Follow the clear path ahead, go

Lotherton Hall

through a gate and keep ahead under an avenue of trees to a crossroads. Turn right **A**, in the Coburnhill Wood and Hook Moor direction, and walk along a pleasant, grassy tree-lined track, which emerges from the trees and continues along the right-hand edge of fields, winding across open country to reach a public footpath sign.

Turn right to continue along a track, parallel to the A1, and go through a gate onto a road **B**. Turn left to pass under two road bridges, take the first road on the right, signposted to Aberford, and walk along the straight road for $\frac{3}{4}$ mile (1.2km) as far as the edge of Aberford, passing some ornate Gothic almshouses, built in 1844. Keep ahead if you want to visit the village – it has some fine Georgian houses, a Victorian church and a pub – but the route continues to the right along Lotherton Lane **C**.

Just after passing under the A1, turn left into Stocking Lane. This narrow lane curves right, and you keep along it for just over $\frac{1}{2}$ mile (800m) to where it passes through a line of trees and bears slightly left. Turn right here **D** over a stile and walk along a track beside an earthwork on the right, possibly part of the defences of the ancient British kingdom of Elmet. Climb a stile, keep ahead gently uphill to a lane, turn right and take the first lane on the left **E**, signposted to Sherburn in Elmet.

Where the lane curves left, turn right along a tarmac drive, at a public footpath sign to Old Micklefield, to re-enter the grounds of Lotherton Hall. The drive leads back to the start. ●

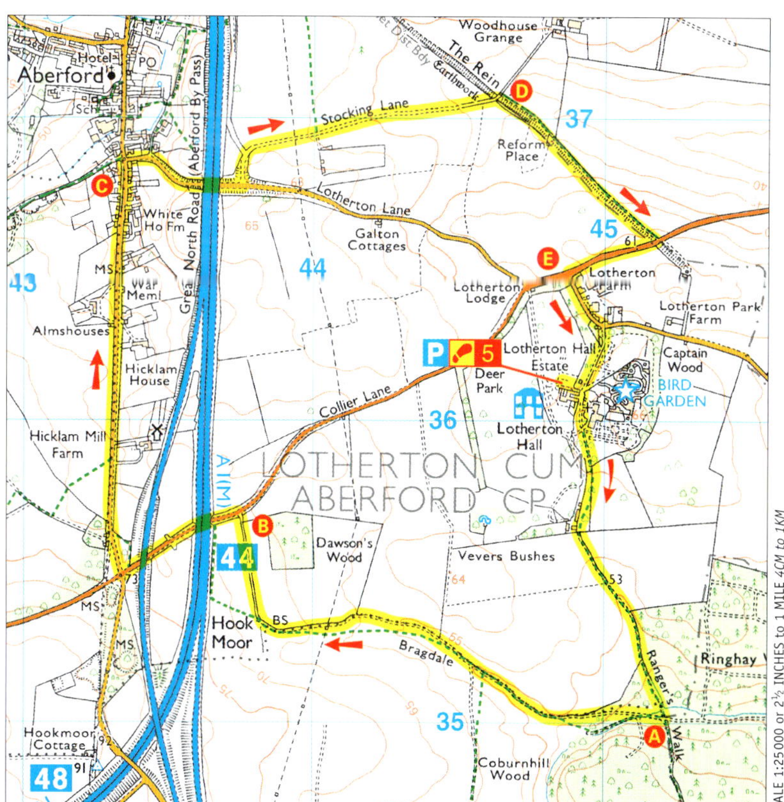

Scale bar: 0 200 400 600 800 METRES 1 KILOMETRE / MILES · 0 200 400 600 YARDS ½

Humber Estuary

Start	Humber Bridge Country Park
Distance	5½ miles (8.9km)
Approximate time	2½ hours
Parking	Humber Bridge Country Park
Refreshments	Café at Country Park, pub at Hessle Foreshore
Ordnance Survey maps	Landranger 106 (Market Weighton), Explorer 293 (Kingston upon Hull & Beverley)

This is mainly a 'there and back' walk along the north shore of the Humber Estuary from the Humber Bridge to North Ferriby. The going is flat and easy but be prepared for some invigorating breezes to come sweeping across the river. The wide views across the estuary to the Lincolnshire side are inevitably dominated by the soaring elegance of the bridge itself.

The Humber Bridge, a marvel of 20th-century engineering, is one of the most impressive structures of its kind and one of the longest single-span suspension bridges in the world. The length of the main span is 4,626ft (1,410m). It took nine years to build and was opened in 1981. The Country Park, comprising around 50 acres (20 ha) of attractive woodland and meadows, was created from a disused chalk quarry.

Start in front of the café and, with your back to it, turn right and take the tarmac path through trees signposted 'Humber Bridge Country Park, Bridge Pedestrian'. Cross one path, bear left along the second one and, at a

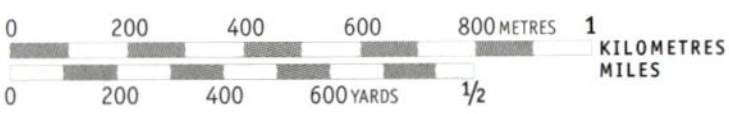

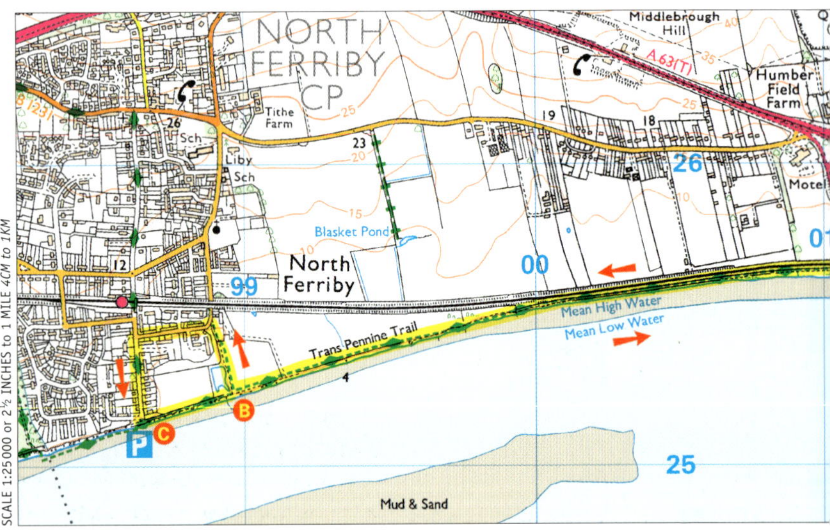

The Humber Bridge

fork, take the right-hand path, signposted 'Country Park Entrance'. After passing through a fence gap, head towards the bridge and, at the next fork, turn right and go through a kissing-gate.

Descend steps through the woodland of the country park and, following signs to Hessle Foreshore, keep ahead to pass first under a railway bridge and then under a road bridge to reach the banks of the Humber **A**. To the right is a disused windmill. Turn right along a tarmac drive and, at public footpath,

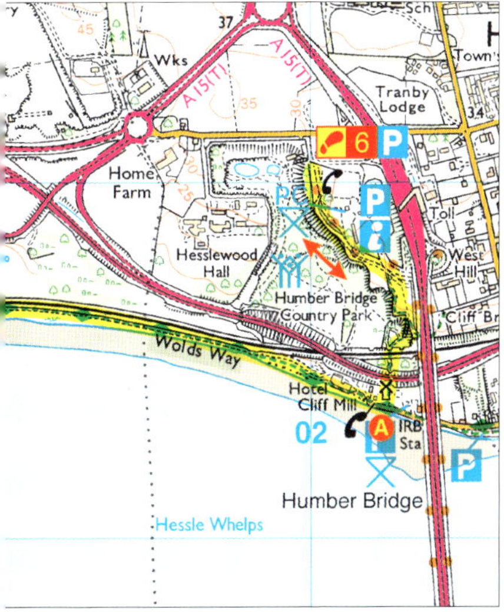

Trans-Pennine Trail and Wolds Way signs, pass through a fence gap and head down to the stony foreshore.

Walk along it, soon joining a path that keeps above it, to reach a stile. Bear slightly left and continue along an embankment to a kissing-gate. Not only are there grand views across and up the river at this point but to the right the southern slopes of the wolds can be seen.

Go through the kissing-gate and keep ahead to the next one, where you turn right **B** at a public footpath sign, along a path away from the river. Go through another kissing-gate, onto a road on the edge of North Ferriby, and turn left. At a T-junction, turn left again to return to the foreshore.

Where the road bends right, descend steps and then turn left along the foreshore **C**. Keep past the first fingerpost and, about 100 yds (91m) farther on, ascend some concrete steps onto an embankment and continue along it to a kissing-gate. After going through it, you rejoin the outward route at point **B** and retrace your steps to the start. On this return stretch, there are particularly superb views of the Humber Bridge in front of you all the while. ●

Kirkham Priory and the River Derwent

Start	Kirkham, parking area in front of priory
Distance	5 miles (8km)
Approximate time	2½ hours
Parking	Kirkham Priory
Refreshments	Pub about ¼ mile (400m) to the east of the start, coffee shop at plant centre by Kirkham Bridge
Ordnance Survey maps	Landranger 100 (Malton & Pickering), Explorer 300 (Howardian Hills & Malton)

The first half of the walk is through woodland, across fields and along lanes above the west side of the Derwent valley. After heading across to the bank of the river, the rest of the route is along a delightful, tree-lined riverside path. There are fine views across the Vale of York to the edge of the wolds and the Howardian Hills. Towards the end, the ruins of Kirkham Priory are seen on the opposite bank of the Derwent. Expect parts of the riverside path to be muddy after wet weather.

The extensive ruins of Kirkham Priory stand in a lovely position above the River Derwent. It was an Augustinian priory, founded in 1125 and suppressed by Henry VIII in 1539. Parts of the church and monastic buildings remain but the major surviving building is the ornate, late 13th-century gatehouse.

Begin by turning left along the road and crossing first Kirkham Bridge over the River Derwent and secondly a railway line. At a public footpath sign, turn left over a stile **A** and take a steep uphill path through Oak Cliff Wood to emerge onto a road. Turn left and, at a public footpath sign, turn left through a gate **B** and walk along a track by the edge of the woodland on the left. After climbing a stile, the path continues through the trees to another stile at the far end.

Kirkham Bridge and the River Derwent

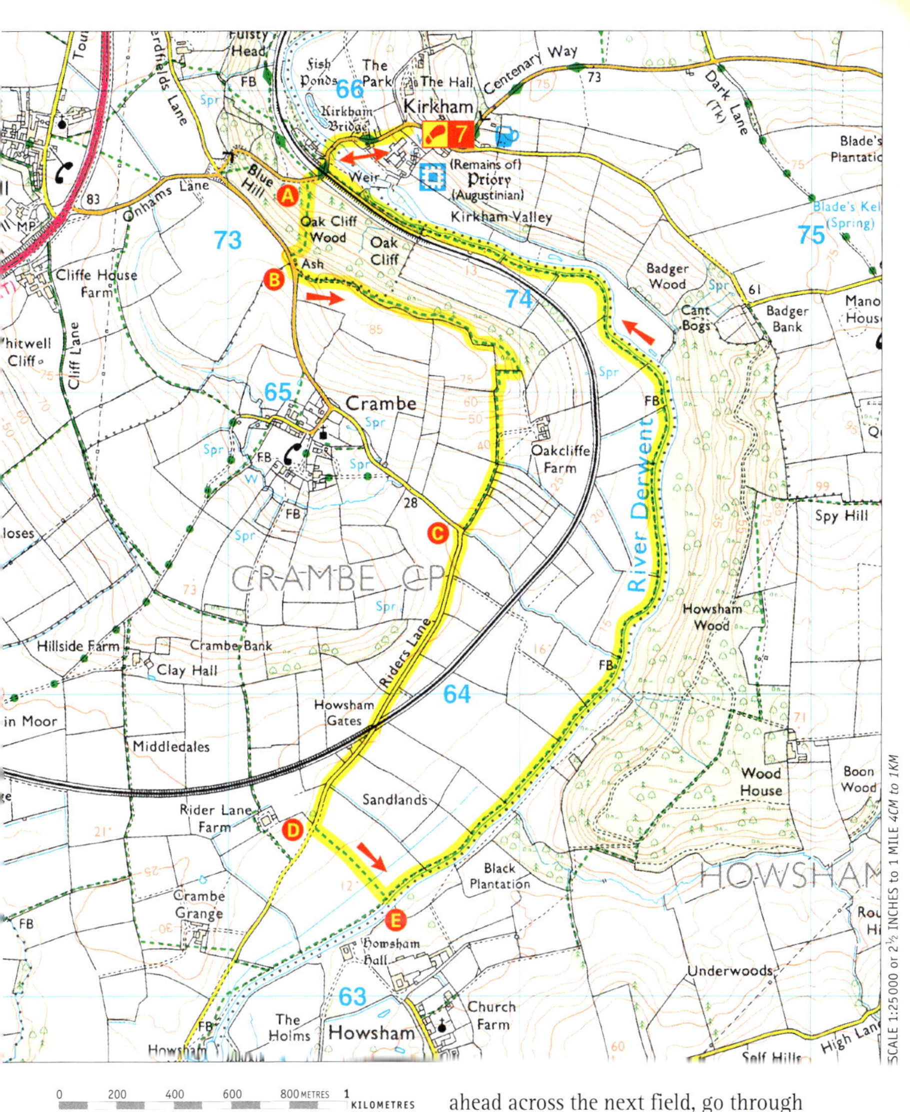

Climb it, turn right along the right-hand edge of a field and, in the corner, turn left to continue along the right edge, heading downhill to join a track. Climb two more stiles and, on reaching a lane **C**, turn left. At a public footpath sign about ¼ mile (400m) beyond a level-crossing, turn left **D**, follow a path across a field – the way is marked by a line of short, white-topped posts – and climb a stile on the far side. Ahead is a view of Howsham Hall and church on the opposite side of the river. Keep ahead across the next field, go through a gate, cross a footbridge over a ditch and continue across the next field.

After going through a gate on the far side, turn left onto a path beside the Derwent **E** and follow the river back to Kirkham Bridge. The route is pleasantly tree-lined. There are several footbridges and stiles, and the terrain is mainly a mixture of woodland and meadow. Sections of the path are likely to be muddy and boggy, and there are boardwalks in places.

Finally, go through a kissing-gate onto the road by Kirkham Bridge and turn right over it to return to the start. ●

Tockwith and the River Nidd

Start	Tockwith
Distance	5½ miles (8.9km)
Approximate time	2½ hours
Parking	Roadside parking at Tockwith
Refreshments	Pubs at Tockwith
Ordnance Survey maps	Landranger 105 (York & Selby), Explorer 289 (Leeds)

Most of this walk is along tracks and field paths between the village of Tockwith and the meandering River Nidd. The middle stretch follows the Nidd around one of its meanders. There are wide views across the Vale of York and, towards the end, the route passes close to the Civil War battlefield of Marston Moor.

The walk starts in the centre of Tockwith at a junction of roads and by the two village pubs. Turn along Westfield Road, signposted to Cattal and Cowthorpe, passing the small Victorian church. Follow the road around a right bend – it now becomes Fleet Lane – and, where it curves left, turn right at a public bridleway sign, along a straight tarmac track **A**.

At a public footpath sign, turn left along a hedge-lined track, which later curves right to reach a gate in front of a barn. Do not go through it but turn right to continue along the hedge-lined track that bears left to a kissing-gate. Go through, walk diagonally across a field to go through another one in the far right-hand corner and keep ahead across the next field – later by a hedge on the right – towards an embankment. Go through a kissing-gate, climb the embank-ment and turn right to walk above the River Nidd **B**.

The River Nidd near Tockwith

As you follow the river around a horseshoe bend – climbing several stiles – there are extensive views across the Vale of York, and the Saxon church at Kirk Hammerton can be seen to the left. Soon after passing an old mill on the opposite bank, you reach a double stile. Climb the first stile and then turn right **C** along a narrow, fence-lined path to a gate. Go through and continue along a hedge-lined track, which bends left to a T-junction.

Turn right along a tarmac track, take the first track on the left, going through a gate, and the track (Moor Lane) runs in a straight line along the top of an embankment to another gate. After going through it, turn right **D** along a track (Kendal Lane). Over to the left is a view of the fields across which the Battle of Marston Moor was fought in 1644. This was one of the most decisive battles of the Civil War and clearly demonstrated the superiority of Cromwell's well-disciplined troops.

The rough track becomes first a tarmac track and then a lane and continues to a T-junction. Turn right back into Tockwith.

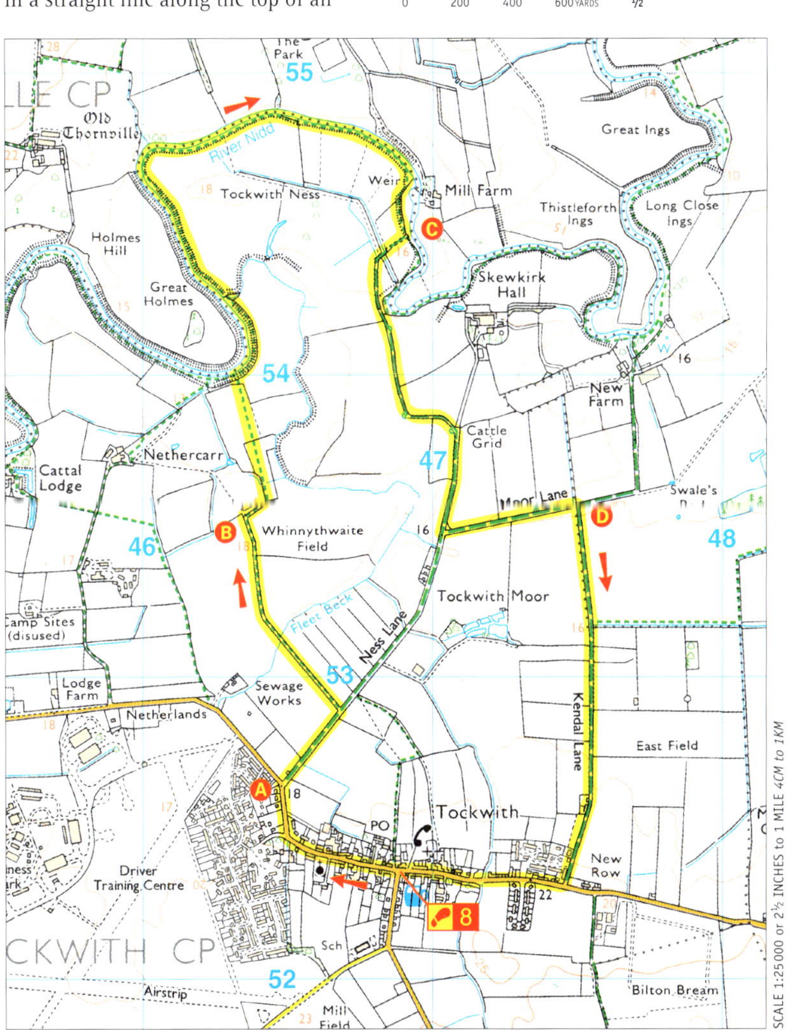

Millington Dale

Start	Millington Wood, on minor road between Millington and Huggate
Distance	5 miles (8km). Shorter version 3½ miles (5.6km)
Approximate time	2½ hours (1½ hours for shorter walk)
Parking	Millington Wood
Refreshments	Pub and café (limited opening) at Millington
Ordnance Survey maps	Landranger 106 (Market Weighton), Explorer 294 (Market Weighton & Yorkshire Wolds Central)

After an opening stretch along a lane on the western side of Millington Dale into the village of Millington, the route heads uphill and continues above the eastern side. You enjoy grand views across the dale before descending and returning to the start. The full walk includes a pleasant stroll through Millington Wood to a fine viewpoint. The route might be muddy on the outward section.

Begin by turning right out of the car park along a narrow, winding lane to Millington village, a distance of about one mile (1.6km). Keep ahead at a crossroads and take the next lane on the left Ⓐ into the village centre, passing to the right of the small but attractive Norman church.

Turn left at a T-junction and, just after the lane bends left, turn right at a Minster Way sign, along the right-hand of two tracks immediately ahead.

Head gently downhill, go through a gate and the track curves right to continue downhill between trees. Where it curves left to a house, keep ahead along an enclosed path to a stile. Climb it – it is likely to be muddy here but

Millington Dale

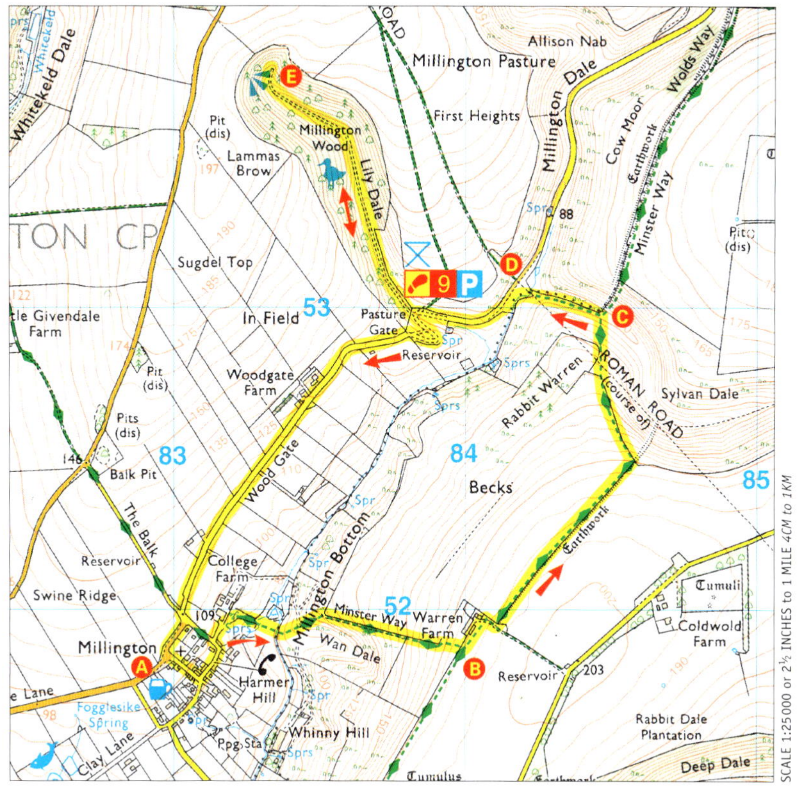

there are some boards – bear slightly left and head uphill across a field, making for a gate.

Do not go through the gate but turn right along a track which continues uphill to a stile. Climb it and head uphill along the left-hand edge of fields, climbing two stiles. After the second stile, turn left **B** along a path by the left-hand edge of a field. Keep to the right of a farm, turn right onto a track and immediately turn left, at a Wolds Way sign, along a path that keeps by the right-hand edge of a field. There are spectacular views to the left over Millington Dale and the surrounding wolds. Millington Wood stands out clearly, confined within the steep slopes of a tributary dale, one of the few remaining wooded dales in the Yorkshire Wolds.

Head downhill and in the field corner bend left to continue along the right-hand edge. Now come superb views to the right down Sylvan Dale. In the next corner, turn right over a stile. Descend steeply, skirting the right-hand edge of a circle of trees and bushes, and continue down to a footpath post at the bottom of the dale **C**. Turn left, keeping by a fence on the right, and look out for where you climb a waymarked stile and continue along a narrow, enclosed path to cross a footbridge over Millington Beck. Keep ahead along a track to a lane **D** and turn left to return to the start.

For the full walk, take the main path through the wood, going through a gate, following the path along the bottom of the dale. Climb the steps and curve left to reach a fine viewpoint **E**, looking back over the trees and Millington Dale to the wolds. From here retrace your steps to the start.

North Cliff and Filey Brigg

Start	Filey, The Crescent. Alternatively start at North Cliff Country Park and follow route directions from point **E**
Distance	5 miles (8km). 4 miles (6.4km) for the shorter version that starts from the Country Park
Approximate time	2½ hours (2 hours for shorter walk)
Parking	Filey, or North Cliff Country Park
Refreshments	Pubs and cafés at Filey, café at North Cliff Country Park
Ordnance Survey maps	Landranger 101 (Scarborough), Explorer 301 (Scarborough, Bridlington & Flamborough Head)

The superb coastal views from North Cliff extend across the sweeping curve of Filey Bay to Flamborough Head. This is an easy route but includes some fine cliff walking. It takes you along the promontory of Filey Brigg and passes close to Filey's medieval church. The shorter walk, which begins at North Cliff Country Park, omits the town.

With its fine and extensive sandy beach and grand views across to Flamborough Head, the old fishing village of Filey became a popular resort in Victorian times, especially after the coming of the railway. Despite this, it never became another Scarborough or Bridlington and has remained fairly small and managed, retaining a pleasing air of gentility and elegance. Nowhere is this elegance more apparent than at the Crescent – where the walk begins – one of the finest in the country and developed by John Wilkes Unett, a Birmingham solicitor, between 1835 and 1850.

Start by the bandstand and, facing the sea, turn left. Where the road bends left into the town centre, keep ahead, in the Coble Landing direction, along a path through gardens and down steps to a road. Turn right towards the sea and turn left along the promenade to the Coble Landing **A**, usually dotted with fishing boats. Follow the road to the left through a wooded ravine (Church Ravine), heading up to a T-junction by the entrance to North Cliff Country Park, and turn left. Keep along the road signposted to Scarborough for about ½ mile (800m) and, at a public footpath sign by the last of the houses, turn right along a straight track **B**.

The track continues along the left-hand edge of a field and, about 50 yds (46m) after following it around a left-hand bend, turn right onto a path that heads gently uphill, by a ditch on the left. Later the path broadens into a track that continues between fields to a T-junction in front of a low embankment **C**. Beyond the embankment, the cliffs plunge steeply to the North Sea.

Turn right and walk along the top of North Cliff to where the main path bends right to a prominent stone marking the junction of the Wolds Way and Cleveland Way. You can keep along this main path and, just beyond the stone, turn right along a clear and well-surfaced path to return to the start but it is worthwhile to keep ahead, along the cliff top, and turn left onto this well-surfaced path a little farther on. This takes you along the promontory of Filey Brigg, an exhilarating walk with the cliffs dropping away steeply on both sides and grand views all around. At the end of the cliffs **D** you can, if you wish, descend to the rocks and continue along to the tip of the Brigg. Otherwise retrace your steps, keeping on the main path as it curves gradually left, giving

magnificent views across the broad sands of Filey Bay to Flamborough Head.

Just before reaching a gate, bear left to continue along the grassy cliff top to reach the edge of a ravine. At the time of writing, the steps down into it and up the other side are closed and the route continues to the right to the North Cliff Country Park café and shop. Turn left in front of it and turn left again **E** onto a tarmac path, which passes to the left of a children's play area.

This is where the walk starts, if doing the shorter version.

SCALE 1:25 000 or 2½ INCHES to 1 MILE 4CM to 1KM

Continue along the left edge of an open, grassy area to rejoin the cliff top and turn right along it. On entering trees on the edge of Church Ravine, descend steps to a tarmac path. If you wish to visit St Oswald's Church, turn right at this point. This sturdy-looking, battlemented, cruciform church was built mainly between 1180 and 1230 and is an interesting example – rare in a small and fairly isolated village church – of the Transitional style when elements of the Gothic form began to appear in Norman architecture.

The route continues to the left along a path that zigzags down the side of the ravine – via a series of steps – to the road Ⓐ. Turn right for the short walk, but if doing the full walk, turn left to pick up the outward route and retrace your steps to the starting point of the walk in Filey.

The Crescent at Filey

Ripon and the rivers Skell and Ure

Start	Ripon, Market Place
Distance	5½ miles (8.9km)
Approximate time	2½ hours
Parking	Ripon
Refreshments	Pubs and cafés at Ripon
Ordnance Survey maps	Landranger 99 (Northallerton & Ripon), Explorer 299 (Ripon & Boroughbridge)

From several points on this undemanding walk, there are distant views of Ripon Cathedral. There is also much attractive walking beside the banks of the rivers Skell and Ure, which meet just to the east of Ripon, partly through woodland and partly across meadows. The middle section of the route is across fields and along a track leading to the village of Sharow.

Ripon has been a major ecclesiastical centre since the 7th century, when a church was founded here by the Northumbrian St Wilfrid. It is the only English cathedral to retain any Saxon architecture – the crypt of the original church. The present building is a mixture of styles and mostly dates from the 13th to 15th centuries. It was a collegiate church of the Archbishops of York and was raised to cathedral status in 1836. One of the more unassuming of English cathedrals, its most distinctive features, apart from the Saxon crypt, are the rows of lancet windows on the 13th-century west front, the imposing east window and the intricate carvings on the 15th-century choir stalls.

The walk starts in the Market Place. Facing the 18th-century town hall, turn left along Kirkgate to the cathedral and turn right down Bedern Bank to a roundabout. Keep ahead along King Street and, after crossing a bridge over the River Skell, turn left A onto a tarmac path beside it. To the right is the Hospital and Chapel of St John the Baptist, founded in 1109.

In front of the next bridge, turn left down steps, turn right to go under the bridge and continue beside the river, passing in front of the Water Rat pub to emerge onto a road. Keep ahead, go under the bypass and, where the road ends, continue along a tree-lined path to the confluence of the Skell and the Ure. The path bends right to continue along the tree-lined banks of the Ure, later turning right away from the river and bending left to emerge from the trees.

Cross a track, keep ahead along the top of a low embankment, continue along the left-hand edge of a field and climb steps onto a road by Hewick Bridge. Turn left over the bridge and, at a public footpath sign to Sharow, turn left again B to walk along the base of

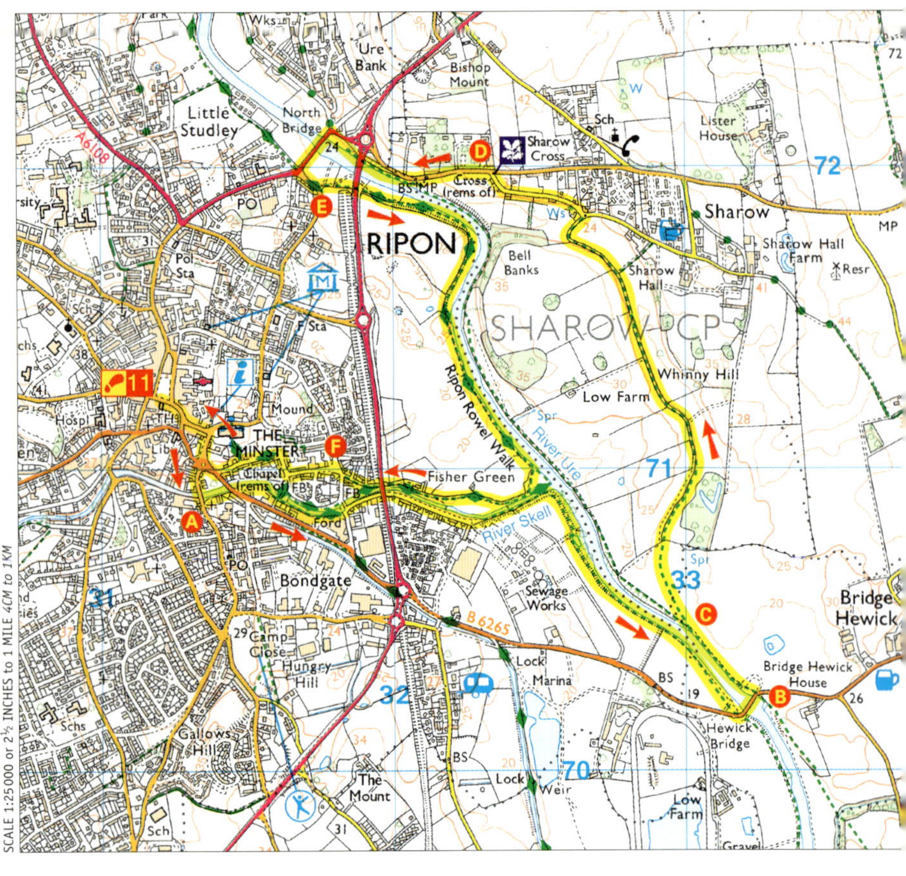

an embankment. Continue by the river along the left-hand edge of a field and after nearly ¼ mile (400m) – where the path bears slightly left – bear right **C** and head across the field, making for the left-hand edge of the trees in front. Go through a metal gate in the hedge on the far side, turn right along the right-hand field edge and, about 50 yds (46m) before reaching the field corner, bear slightly right to continue along an enclosed track.

Keep along this winding track for just over ½ mile (800m) – there are attractive views to the right of the houses and church tower of Sharow – and the track eventually bends right and goes through a gate to reach a lane. Turn left to a T-junction by Sharow

Cross **D**. In the Middle Ages there were eight of these crosses around Ripon but this is the only one to survive. The crosses marked the boundary of the area – within one mile (1.6km) of the church at Ripon – where sanctuary could be obtained.

At the cross, turn left along a road and, approaching a roundabout, bear slightly left to continue along a tarmac cycleway and footpath. Pass under a road bridge and keep ahead to a T-junction. Turn left over North Bridge, turn left again along Magdalen's Road and, where it bends right, turn left **E** along a track to a kissing-gate.

Go through, follow a path under the road bridge again and continue across delightful riverside meadows beside the Ure, following the river around a right curve. After going through a kissing-gate, keep ahead through a belt of trees and continue between a wire fence on the right and the trees bordering the river on the left. Go through two more gates and, after the second of these, bear right across the meadow to the banks of the River Skell. Continue alongside the river. At a fork, take the right-hand path along the right edge of a meadow, rejoin the Skell at the far, tapering end and keep beside it to a kissing-gate.

Go through, continue along a path to join a track, pass under a road bridge and keep ahead to the end of a road.

Walk along the road, keep ahead at a crossroads **F** – by the side of a small triangular green – and continue along Low Mill Road. Follow the road around a right-hand bend and take the first road on the left (High Street Agnesgate), passing to the right of the 15th-century ruins of the chapel of St Anne's. At a T-junction, turn right to a roundabout and then turn right again up Bedern Bank, here rejoining the outward route. From here retrace your steps to the starting point of the walk at the Market Place.

Ripon Cathedral

Howden Marsh and the River Ouse

Start	Howden
Distance	6½ miles (10.5km)
Approximate time	3 hours
Parking	Howden
Refreshments	Pubs and cafés at Howden, pub by Boothferry Bridge
Ordnance Survey maps	Landrangers 105 (York & Selby) or 106 (Market Weighton), Explorer 291 (Goole & Gilberdyke)

After a short circuit of Howden Marsh on the edge of the town, the route continues along roads and tracks to reach the banks of the River Ouse just to the west of Boothferry Bridge. For the next two miles (3.2km) you walk along an embankment above the river before returning to Howden. There are wide and open views from the embankment, with the tower of Howden Minster in sight for much of the way.

The medieval bishops of Durham were the lords of the manor of Howden and responsible for the town's chief glories. Dominating the pleasant Market Square is the minster, a large collegiate church built mainly between 1265 and 1330. Its tall central tower is particularly impressive. After the religious upheavals of the 16th century, the east end and chapter house became ruined, and the minster became a parish church. Nearby is the former manor house of the bishops of Durham, passed at the end of the walk.

🐾 Start in the Market Place and, facing the minster, take the paved path to the right of it (Churchside) which emerges onto a road by the west front. Continue along the road opposite (St John's Street) and, where it ends just to the left of a fork, keep ahead along a path to enter Howden Marsh. Like the town, this attractive and tranquil area of woodland and marsh – considerably larger in the Middle Ages than now – belonged to the bishops of Durham. It is now a valuable recreational amenity.

Follow the path – there are duckboards in places – to a T-junction in front of a pool, turn right alongside the pool and keep ahead to climb steps into woodland. Turn left along a tree-lined path – part of a disused railway track – and, at a T-junction, turn left to

Howden Minster

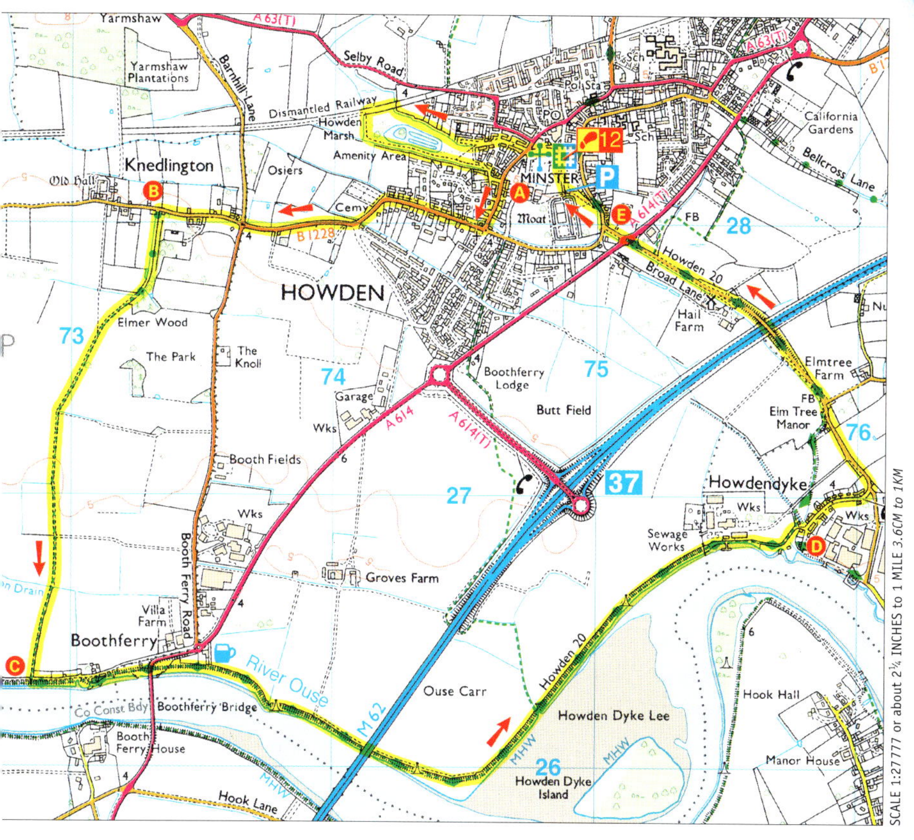

keep along the right-hand edge of the marsh, by a drainage channel on the right. The path curves left, and you keep along it – ignoring all side turns to the left – to a T-junction. Turn right along a track, turn left along a road to another T-junction and turn right Ⓐ.

At a crossroads turn right again, in the Goole direction, along Knedlington Road and keep ahead at the next crossroads into Knedlington. At a public footpath sign, turn left Ⓑ along a track, initially by the right edge of woodland but later across fields. Drax power-station can be seen to the right and Boothferry Bridge to the left. Follow the track to the base of an embankment, climb it and turn left Ⓒ to continue above the broad waters of the River Ouse.

Keep beside the river for the next two miles (3.2km), climbing several stiles and passing under first Boothferry Bridge and then the bridge that carries the M62 across the Ouse. Eventually, the path reaches a tarmac drive by a works. Keep ahead along a track in front of the works, which curves first left and then bears right over a brick bridge to a road at Howdendyke Ⓓ. Turn left, at a T-junction turn left again and follow the road over the motorway into Howden. Keep ahead at a crossroads to a T-junction and turn right along Hailgate.

For a pleasant finale, turn left through iron gates into Ashes Playing Fields Ⓔ and turn right along a tarmac path, passing a children's play area, to a T-junction. Turn right, go through a gate and follow a path to the left of the Bishop's Manor house, which leads back to the Market Place.

Welburn and Castle Howard

Start	Welburn, by the post office
Distance	5½ miles (8.9km)
Approximate time	2½ hours
Parking	Roadside parking at Welburn
Refreshments	Pub at Welburn
Ordnance Survey maps	Landranger 100 (Malton & Pickering), Explorer 300 (Howardian Hills & Malton)

Almost the whole of this walk is across the parkland and through some of the woodlands of the Castle Howard estate on the northern fringes of the Vale of York. There are distant views of the great house, and the route passes close to some of the other buildings that form part of the park's landscape. There are also wide views across to the Howardian Hills and the edge of the Yorkshire Wolds. The route is undemanding and easy to follow.

With your back to the post office, turn right and then left along Water Lane. Where the road ends, continue along a track. At a crossroads, keep ahead across a field towards woodland and go through a gate to enter the wood.

Descend to cross a footbridge over Moorhouse Beck, bear left and head up through the trees to join a track. Go through a gate and keep ahead to a T-junction **A**. From here there are fine views of low hills and woodlands. Some of the striking monuments that adorn the parkland of Castle Howard can also be seen. To the right is the Mausoleum and to the left the Pyramid, both built in the early 18th century and roughly contemporary with the house.

Turn left at the T-junction. Almost immediately, turn right along a path and cross a high-arched bridge, built in 1744 over New River Pond. It is at this point that you get the best and closest view of the great domed house of Castle Howard, one of England's finest stately homes, built in the early 18th century for Charles Howard, third Earl of Carlisle. It was designed by Vanbrugh and Hawksmoor, who were

The bridge over New River Pond

also responsible for most of the monuments in the park. Nearer at hand is the impressive Temple of the Four Winds.

After going through a gate, the route continues ahead across grass over the brow of a low hill, making for the corner of a wire fence in a dip. At this point, bear left across the field to join a track and bear right along it, by a wall on the left. Climb a stile to the left of a gate, continue through trees to a T-junction and turn right **B**. The track winds across parkland, crosses a bridge over Mill Hills Beck and continues through trees to a T-junction in front of a barn.

Turn right, follow the track through farm buildings and continue across the park. The track bends right in front of a barn and, at a T-junction, turn right **C** to continue along a tarmac track. At a Centenary Way sign, turn left **A** to briefly rejoin the outward route but, after going through a gate into woodland, turn left off the outward route and walk along a track by the left, inside edge of the wood. Later the track continues through Pretty Wood towards the Four Faces, a whimsical monument built in 1737. Just before reaching it, turn right **D** at a Centenary Way sign, along a track that curves right and heads downhill to a stile.

Climb it, keep ahead uphill along the right, inside edge of the trees, go

through a gate and continue uphill by the left-hand edge of a field. To the right is an attractive view of Welburn village and its Victorian church. Climb a stile and, at a T-junction, turn right along a track. Go through a gate, keep ahead to emerge onto a road **E** and turn right into Welburn.

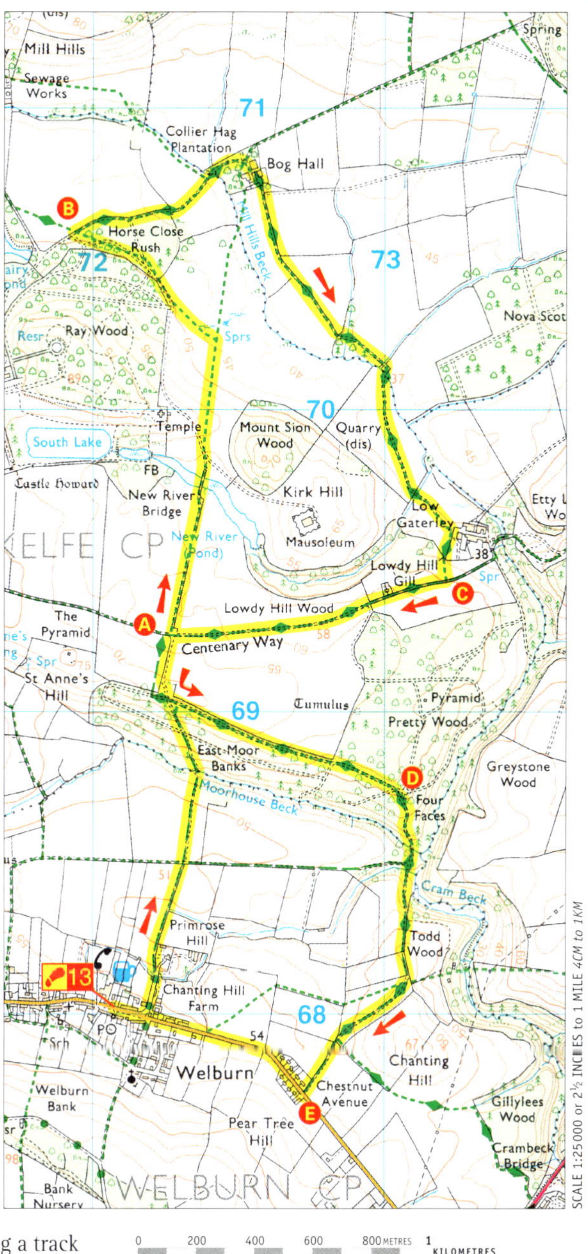

Newbald Wold

Start	North Newbald
Distance	5½ miles (8.9km)
Approximate time	3 hours
Parking	North Newbald, around the Green
Refreshments	Pubs at North Newbald
Ordnance Survey maps	Landranger 106 (Market Weighton), Explorer 293 (Kingston upon Hull & Beverley)

Almost the whole of the walk is in open country, providing a series of extensive views, both across the wolds and over the Vale of York. The route could hardly be more straightforward: over Newbald Wold, through a dry valley, back over the wold into Swin Dale and return to the start. North Newbald is an appealing village with two pubs and a fine Norman church.

The spacious village of North Newbald is noted for its superb Norman cruciform church, built around 1140 and restored in the 19th century.

Begin by heading towards the church, passing between the two village pubs. Keep to the right of the church and continue along Galegate to a T-junction. Turn right along Townside Road and, at a public footpath sign opposite Townside Close, turn left along an uphill track **A**.

Follow this track over the brow of the wold and descend into the bottom of the dale to the right of a farm. Turn right **B**, follow a path through the dale bottom to a stile, climb it and keep ahead to climb another one by the right-hand edge of sloping woodland. Continue alongside the wood and by

Near North Newbald

the left-hand edge of fields, following the edge around right and left curves and heading gently uphill to a T-junction **C**.

Turn right along a straight, hedge-lined track, which heads back over the wold, descending to a lane. Turn right and, at a Wolds Way fingerpost, turn left downhill **D** along another enclosed track to a lane. Turn right and, at a Wolds Way sign to South Cave, turn left **E** along a track, go through a gate and the track curves left to continue through Swin Dale. About 100 yds (91m) after the track curves left, look out for where a clear and obvious grassy path leads off sharply to the right and turn onto it **F**. The path heads gently uphill across the field towards a footpath sign on the edge of a young plantation.

Continue quite steeply uphill through the plantation and, at the top, climb a stile and walk along the right-hand edge of a field to a road. Turn right and follow the road downhill into North Newbald.

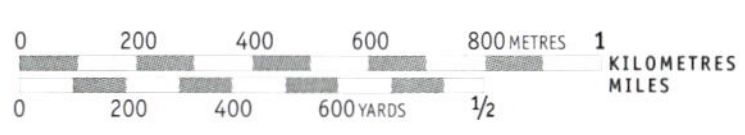

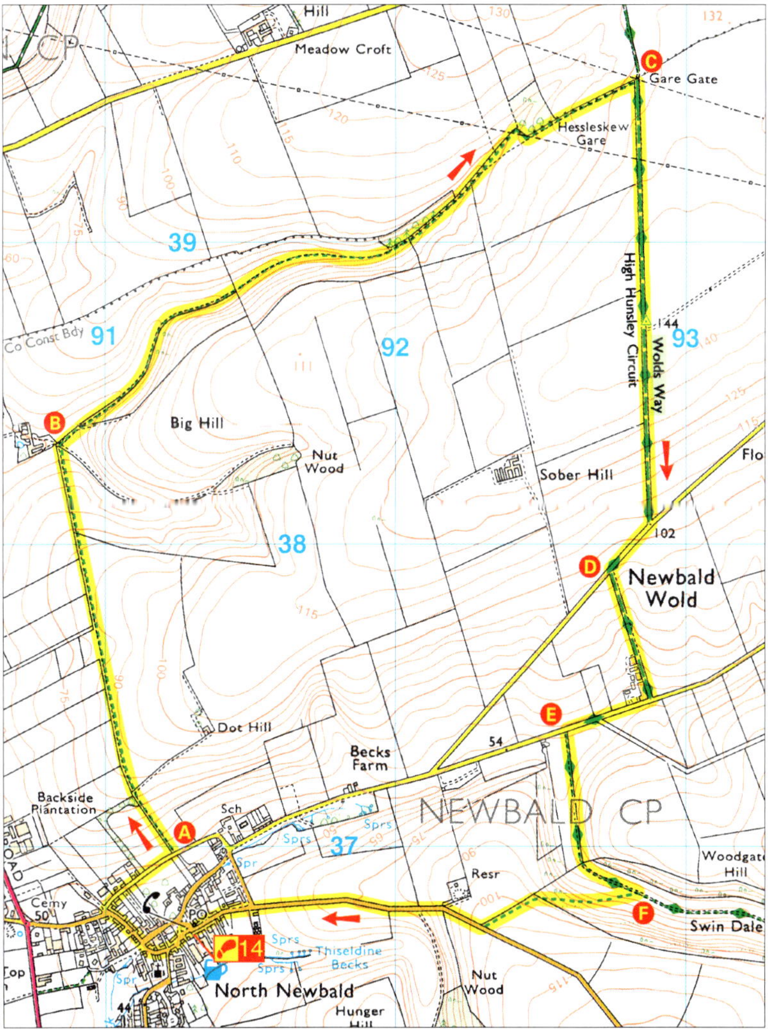

SCALE 1:25 000 or 2½ INCHES to 1 MILE 4CM to 1KM

Flamborough Head

Start	Flamborough Head, South Landing, signposted from Flamborough
Distance	7 miles (11.3km)
Approximate time	3½ hours
Parking	South Landing
Refreshments	Café near lighthouse, pub and café at North Landing, pubs and cafés at Flamborough
Ordnance Survey maps	Landranger 101 (Scarborough), Explorer 301 (Scarborough, Bridlington & Flamborough Head)

Most of this exhilarating route is along exposed clifftop paths around the dramatic chalk cliffs of Flamborough Head, following the headland from South Landing to Thornwick Bay. The final stretch is across the neck of the headland, passing through Flamborough village. Views of the cliffs, especially in the vicinity of the lighthouse, are magnificent. Note that not all the clifftop walking is flat; there are several points where deep gullies that cut into the cliffs necessitate some steep descents and ascents, although most of these have steps.

Flamborough Head is where the Yorkshire Wolds meet the North Sea, the northernmost limit of England's chalk country.

Turn left out of the car park down a lane, beside a wooded ravine on the left, then, at a public footpath sign, turn left down steps **A**. Keep ahead across grass, climb a flight of steps and, at the top, turn right. The path bends left to keep along the top of the cliffs to a fork.

Take the right-hand path, which continues along the top of the cliffs, descending and ascending several flights of steps because of steep inlets and curving gradually left towards the lighthouse. On approaching the two masts of the Fog Signal Station, turn left onto a path along the left-hand edge of a grassy area to a footpath post and turn left along a tarmac track heading directly for the lighthouse.

Just before reaching the lighthouse, bear right onto a path that bends right along the clifftop beside the brick wall of the lighthouse to emerge onto the end of a road. Keep ahead – the tower seen in front is an earlier 17th-century lighthouse – and, when you see a footpath post, turn right **B** across grass, descend steps and then climb back up onto the top of the cliffs. The path keeps along the edge of a golf course, curving left towards North Landing. After bending left, descend steps, curve right to reach the end of a road at North Landing **C** and immediately turn right, at a public footpath sign to Thornwick Bay, onto a path by the right-hand edge of a car park.

At the end of the car park, turn sharp left down a flight of steps, climb a stile at the bottom, turn sharp right, ascend steps, climb another stile and head up to the clifftop again. Climb another stile and, as you continue along the cliffs, there is a superb view ahead of the almost perpendicular Bempton Cliffs. The path bends left above Thornwick Bay and, at a public footpath sign to North Cliff, turn right down steps, climb the other side of the ravine and turn left along a track.

Almost immediately after the track

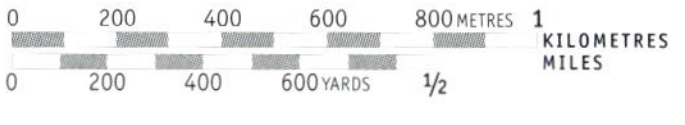

becomes tarmacked, turn right **D** alongside a fence on the left – the path soon becomes fence-lined both sides – making for a house. Turn left in front of it and at a wall corner turn right. Keep ahead to the field corner, turn left, and the way continues across grass parallel to the tarmac drive of a caravan park on the right. Cross a drive, keep ahead along an enclosed and paved path and continue along the right-hand edge of a field to emerge, via a stile, onto a road **E**.

Turn right into Flamborough and keep ahead through the village centre. This attractive farming and fishing village has a sturdy-looking and much restored medieval church with a Norman chancel arch. Just beyond the Dog and Duck pub, turn left along Allison Lane to a T-junction **F**. Turn right, keep ahead at a crossroads, and the road leads back to the start.

Flamborough Head

Watton and Kilnwick

Start	Watton, the Green at the corner of the main road and village street
Distance	7 miles (11.3km)
Approximate time	3½ hours
Parking	By the Green at Watton
Refreshments	None
Ordnance Survey maps	Landranger 106 (Market Weighton), Explorers 294 (Market Weighton & Yorkshire Wolds Central) and 295 (Bridlington, Driffield & Hornsea)

This walk on the eastern fringes of the Yorkshire Wolds includes two small, secluded village churches and passes through the site of a now vanished medieval priory. There are extensive views across the surrounding flat landscape, attractive walking beside becks and pleasant wooded stretches. Some parts of the route are likely to be muddy after wet weather.

Begin by taking the road through Watton, at a public footpath sign, turn left along a hedge-lined, tarmac track to a kissing-gate. Go through, walk across a field, go through another gate on the far side and keep ahead in front of a house to cross Watton Beck.

Turn right **A** onto a path that runs along the top of a low embankment between fields on the left and the beck on the right. Later, you keep along the right-hand edge of woodland, continue past a footbridge and follow the path as it bends left, away from the beck,

Kilnwick church

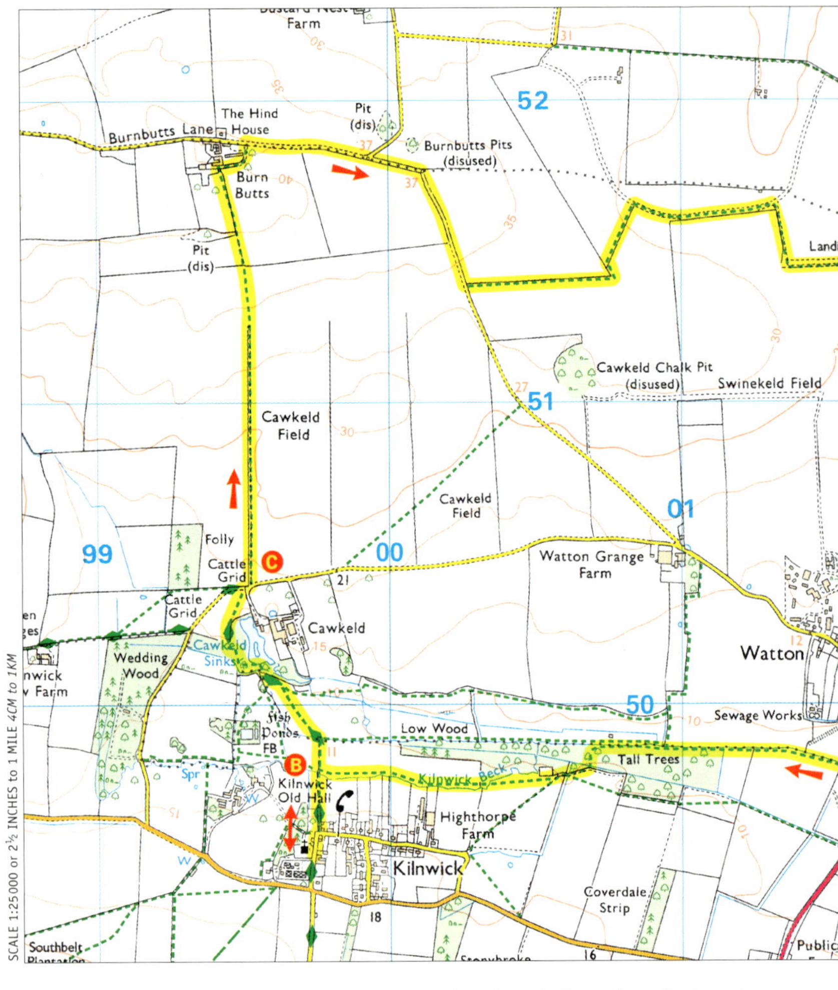

winding through rough grass and trees to a footbridge over Kilnwick Beck. After crossing it, turn right along the right-hand edge of a field, go through a gate in the corner, continue along the right-hand edge of the next field, but look out for where you turn right over another footbridge. The path bends left through woodland, passes beside a gate and continues along the left-hand edge of a field. Kilnwick church can be seen to the left.

At a crossroads by a Minster Way fingerpost **B**, turn left along an enclosed track for a closer look at the stone and brick church. It dates from the Middle Ages but was largely rebuilt in the Victorian era. Return to the fingerpost and keep ahead to climb a stile on the far side of the field. Bear left across the next field towards woodland, continuing past the corner of the trees to a stile. Climb it, follow the path as it bears left through the wood – crossing several plank footbridges – and climb a stile on the far edge of the trees.

Bear right by the right-hand edge of a field and, where the fence bears right, keep ahead to cut across the corner to a lane in front of a Minster Way sign **C**. Turn right and, at a public footpath

continue along the right-hand edge of a field to a T-junction. Turn right along a broad track, turn right onto another track at a waymarked post, follow it around a left-hand bend and keep ahead to go through a kissing-gate onto a main road **D**. Cross over, go through a kissing-gate opposite and walk along the left-hand edge of a field. Later the path bears slightly right, away from the field edge and then bears left to a fingerpost by a footbridge. Do not cross the footbridge but turn right **E**, in the Watton direction, alongside a drain on the left and, after passing between redundant gateposts, turn right and go through a kissing-gate.

Continue along the right-hand edge of a succession of fields and through a series of kissing-gates. In the last field before reaching a farm, the earthworks that can be seen in the field on the right are virtually all that remain of Watton Priory, a small house of the Gilbertine Order. Unusually, it catered for both canons and nuns. In the corner of this last field, turn right, go through two kissing-gates in quick succession and, at the corner of a ruined brick building on the left – a monastic outbuilding thought to date from the 15th or 16th century – keep ahead across the field, making for a kissing-gate on the far side **F**.

Before going through it, turn sharp left and head diagonally across the uneven field – more monastic earthworks – to the attractive, brick-built, 16th-century Watton church, possibly partly built with material from the priory. A kissing-gate by a fence corner admits you to the churchyard, and the large house to the left includes part of the former prior's lodging.

Retrace your steps to the previous kissing-gate, go through and walk along an attractive, tree-lined path to return to the start.

sign, turn left onto a track that runs in a straight line along the left-hand edge of a field. Go through a hedge gap, turn left along the left-hand edge of the next field. The path bends right to continue across the field, later keeping by its left-hand edge towards farm buildings. In the field corner, follow the edge, first to the right and then to the left, to a lane. Turn right along the narrow lane and, at a fork, continue along the right-hand lane. Follow it around a right-hand bend and, at a public footpath sign, turn left through a kissing-gate.

Walk along the left-hand edge of a field, follow the edge as it bends left, go through a fence gap and turn right to

Fridaythorpe and Huggate

Start	Fridaythorpe
Distance	6½ miles (10.5km)
Approximate time	3 hours
Parking	Roadside parking at Fridaythorpe, near the church
Refreshments	Pubs at Fridaythorpe, pub at Huggate
Ordnance Survey maps	Landranger 106 (Market Weighton), Explorer 294 (Market Weighton & Yorkshire Wolds Central)

This outstanding walk takes you across a classic high wolds landscape of open hillsides and steep-sided, narrow dales with extensive and superb views. Over half the route is on the well-waymarked Wolds Way. The attractive villages of Fridaythorpe and Huggate both have interesting churches and appealing pubs, and the brief detour into Huggate is definitely recommended.

Start by the small and secluded Norman church, which is a delightful building in a fine setting overlooking the wolds, and walk along the lane, in the York and Driffield direction, to a T-junction by the Manor House Inn. Turn right along the main road and, where it bends right, bear left at a Wolds Way sign, along a tarmac track. The track becomes a rough enclosed track and, where it curves left, turn right to a footpath post beyond which is a gate **A**.

Go through, bear right – leaving the Wolds Way – and as you continue along the right-hand edge of a field, there is a striking view to the left down Holm Dale, traversed on the return leg. Climb a stile, keep along the right-hand edge of a field and, after passing through a gap into the next field, turn left to continue along its left-hand edge. Follow the track to the right, head across fields towards trees and continue through the farmyard of Wold House Farm, turning left at a yellow waymark in front of a barn and then turning right along a tarmac track.

After about 200 yds (183m), turn left at a waymarked post **B**, and head gently downhill along the left-hand edge of a field to a stile. Climb it, veer right away from the field edge and continue down through a shallow valley into Horse Dale, bearing left to climb another stile. Turn left, head uphill along a track and continue along a grassy ledge above the dale. From here the views are really superb, but do not let them distract you too much for after 200 yds (183m) the route continues to the right through a waymarked gate. Keep along the left-hand edge of a field to a T-junction and turn left along a tarmac track, here rejoining the Wolds Way for the remainder of the walk.

Where the track bears slightly left to a house and farm, keep ahead at a public footpath sign, along an enclosed path that heads downhill to join a

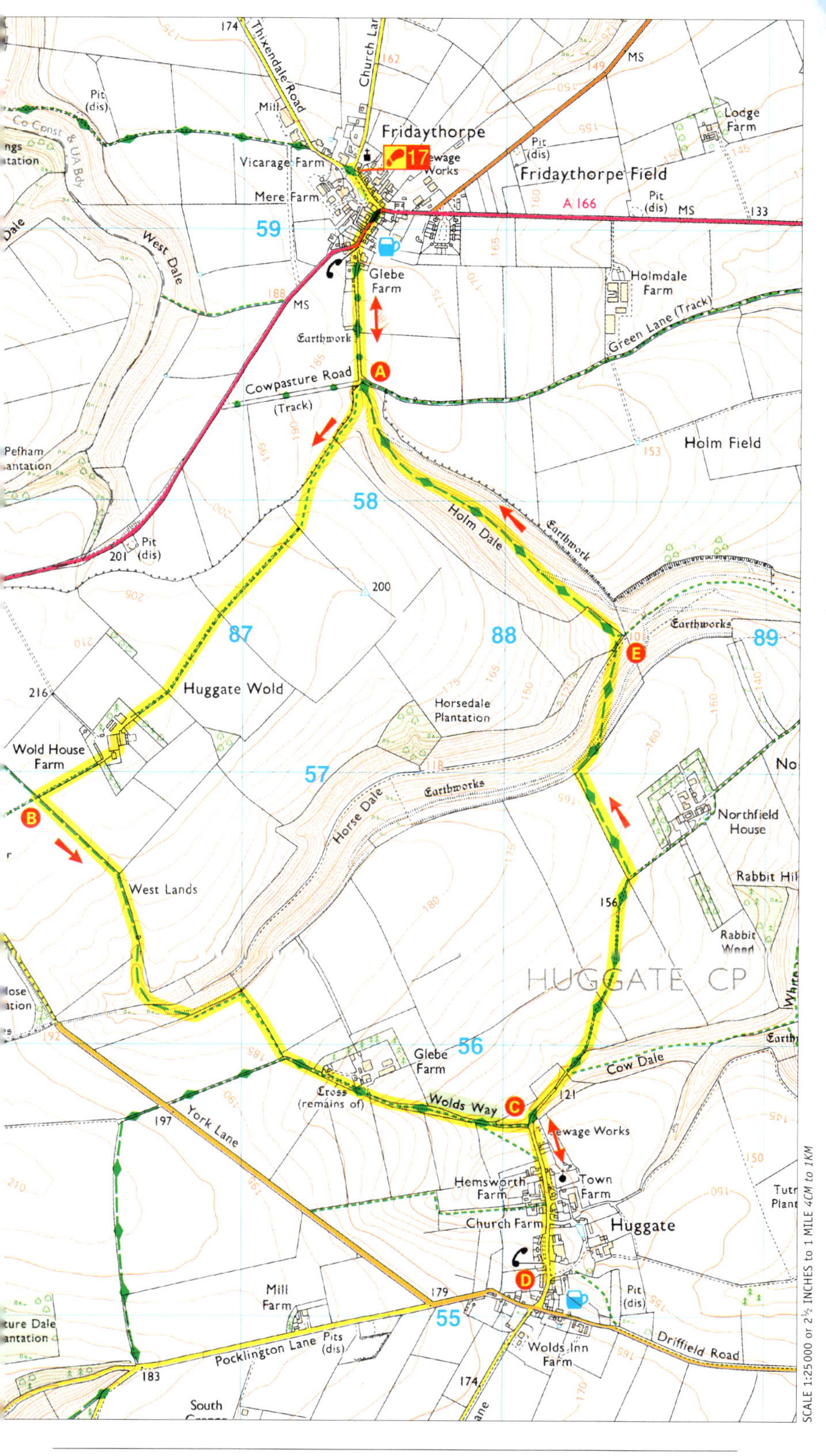

Thixendale Road
Church Lane
Mill
162
174
175
Fridaythorpe
MS
149
150
155
Lodge
Farm
145
Pit
(dis)
Vicarage Farm
Mere Farm
Fridaythorpe Field
Pit
(dis)
160
A 166
133
MS
Co Const & UA Bdy
59
West Dale
188
MS
Holmdale
Farm
Green Lane (Track)
Glebe
Farm
165
170
Earthwork
A
Cowpasture Road
(Track)
Pefham
Plantation
153
Holm Field
200
58
Holm Dale
Earthwork
201
Pit
(dis)
205
210
200
87
Huggate Wold
88
Earthworks
89
216
Horsedale
Plantation
175
165
150
160
140
Wold House
Farm
150
57
Horse Dale
Earthworks
118
B
West Lands
175
180
156
Northfield
House
Rabbit Hill
Rabbit
Wood
HUGGATE CP
192
56
Glebe
Farm
Cow Dale
121
Cross
(remains of)
Wolds Way
C
York Lane
197
Sewage Works
150
145
Hemsworth
Farm
Town
Farm
210
160
Tutt
Plant
Church Farm
Huggate
Mill
Farm
D
179
55
Pocklington Lane
Pits
(dis)
Wolds Inn
Farm
Driffield Road
183
174
170
South
Grange
SCALE 1:25 000 or 2½ INCHES to 1 MILE 4CM to 1KM
17
Earthwork
E
101

Horse Dale

tarmac track. Keep ahead to a T-junction
C and, although the route continues to
the left, it is worth turning right uphill
along a lane for a detour into Huggate
D. There is a good pub, and the church
has a spire on its 14th-century tower
and a fine Norman chancel arch.

Return to the T-junction where you
joined the lane **C** and keep ahead
along it, down into a dip and up again.
The lane becomes the drive to
Northfield Farm and, at a Wolds Way
sign, turn left off it and walk along the
left-hand edge of a field to a gate in the
corner. Go through, turn right to walk
along the ledge you were on earlier
above Horse Dale and, after about
100 yds (91m), look out for a blue-
waymarked post, where you bear left
onto a path that slants downhill across
the slopes of the dale to two stiles at the
bottom **E**.

Climb the stile on the left – there is a
Wolds Way sign – and continue along a
delightful winding path through the
bottom of Holm Dale. At a fork near the
head of the dale, take the right-hand
path up to a gate **A** and go through to
rejoin the outward route. Retrace your
steps to the start.

Harpham, Burton Agnes and Kilham

Start	Bracey Bridge picnic site, off A614 between Driffield and Burton Agnes
Distance	7 miles (11.3km)
Approximate time	3½ hours
Parking	Bracey Bridge picnic site
Refreshments	Kiosk at start, pub at Harpham, pub at Burton Agnes, café at Burton Agnes Hall, pubs at Kilham
Ordnance Survey maps	Landranger 101 (Scarborough), Explorer 295 (Bridlington, Driffield & Hornsea)

This walk across gently undulating country links three attractive villages that lie at the foot of the wolds. All of them have pubs and medieval churches. There are extensive views, and the route passes by Burton Agnes Hall, a fine Elizabethan mansion that is well worth a visit.

On the south side of the picnic site, climb a stile to the right of gates and walk along a wooded track which becomes enclosed. At a fork, take the right-hand track, climb a stile and continue along the right-hand edge of woodland.

At a public footpath sign, climb a stile, keep ahead across the next field, climb another stile and follow the track to the left Ⓐ, crossing a bridge over Lowthorpe Beck. Keep ahead, passing through trees, climb a stile, pass to the left of a farm and go through a gate onto a lane. Turn right into Harpham and walk along Main Street to a crossroads. The medieval church is to the right.

The route continues to the left and, at a public footpath sign, turn right Ⓑ over a stile and walk along an enclosed path to climb another one. Head across a field, climb a stile, continue in the same direction across the next field and,

on the far side, bear right along its left-hand edge. Look out for where you turn left over a stile, head diagonally across a field to a waymarked telegraph pole and bear slightly right to continue across the field to a stile. Climb it, walk across the corner of the next field, climb another stile and continue across a field, making for a footpath sign where you go through a gap to emerge onto a road in Burton Agnes.

Turn right, and the route continues along the first lane on the left, signposted to Rudston Ⓒ. To visit Burton Agnes Hall, Norman House and the church – a fascinating and varied collection of adjacent buildings – take the second lane on the left. The hall is a splendid late-Elizabethan mansion, and is noted for its fine collections of furniture, paintings and china. It also has particularly attractive grounds. The Norman House is the predecessor of the hall, and the later brick exterior

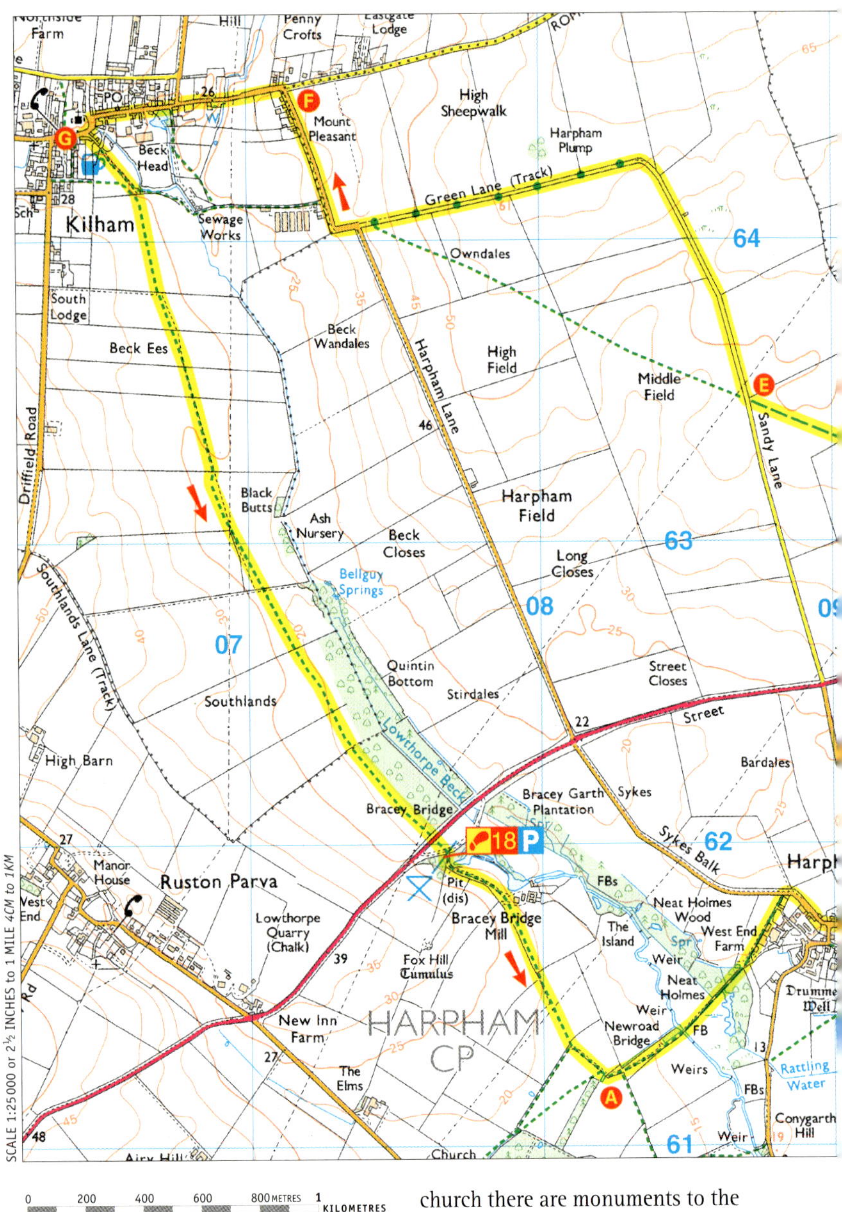

conceals a rare example of a Norman hall. The church, which is approached through an archway of yews, was founded in the 12th century. It retains some of its original Norman work, notably the chancel arch, but dates mainly from the 15th century and has been restored several times. Inside the church there are monuments to the various owners of Burton Agnes Hall.

Retrace your steps to to the lane at Rudston **C** and just over ¼ mile (400m) along the lane turn left **D** at a public footpath sign, along the left-hand edge of a field and, at a fence corner, keep ahead across the field, heading down into a shallow dip and then up to a hedge gap – there is a yellow waymark here. Go through, head

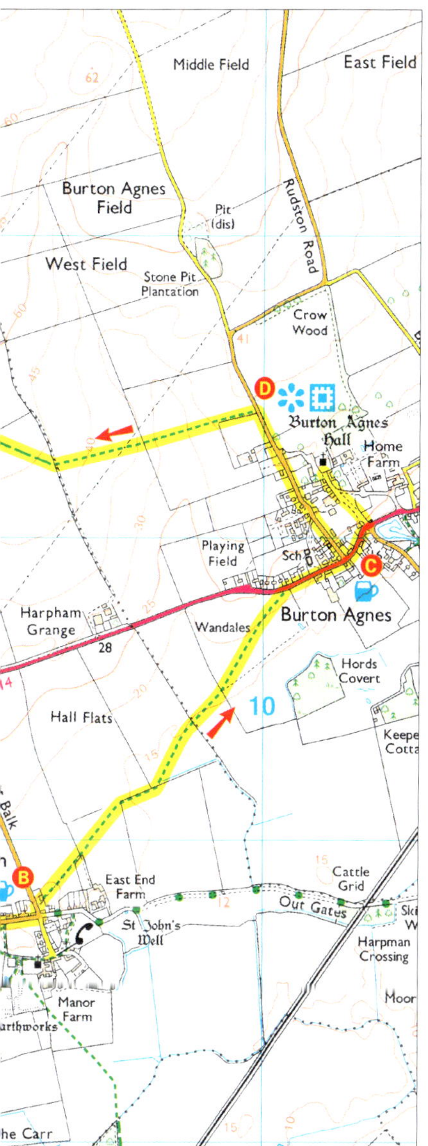

The church and Norman House at Burton Agnes Hall

corner. Keep ahead, follow the lane around a right-hand bend to a T-junction and turn left **F** along East Street into Kilham, once a centre of some importance in the wolds. Just after the lane bends left in front of the impressive medieval church, turn sharp left **G** along a tarmac track (Bakehouse Lane) to a stile. Climb it and bear left diagonally across a field.

Climb a stile in the far corner, and the route continues in more or less a straight line across a succession of fields and through a series of hedge gaps, with occasional stiles. Note that at one point you keep for a short distance along the right-hand edge of a field before continuing as before. Finally, head across to a waymarked post in the corner of a field by the edge of woodland and continue by the right-hand edge of the trees to a stile in front of an embankment.

Climb the stile and the embankment and cross a road. Go through a gap in the trees opposite to return to the Bracey Bridge picnic site. ●

straight across the next field, making for a waymarked post just to the right of a solitary tree, go through a hedge gap and continue across the next two fields, finally climbing a stile onto a narrow lane **E**.

Turn right and, where the tarmac ends, bear left along a grassy track, which curves left and continues as an enclosed track – pleasantly tree-lined on one stretch – to reach a lane at a

Sheriff Hutton and Mowthorpe Hill

Start	Sheriff Hutton, crossroads in village centre
Distance	7 miles (11.3km)
Approximate time	3½ hours
Parking	Roadside parking at Sheriff Hutton
Refreshments	Pubs at Sheriff Hutton
Ordnance Survey maps	Landranger 100 (Malton & Pickering), Explorer 300 (Howardian Hills & Malton)

A walk across fields at the foot of the Howardian Hills is followed by a brief and easy ascent onto the ridge of Mowthorpe Hill. From here there are extensive views over the northern part of the Vale of York. After descending, the return leg follows a more undulating route, and on the final stretch the church and ruined castle at Sheriff Hutton stand out prominently on the low ridge occupied by the village. Some of the field paths are likely to be muddy during wet weather.

The quiet village of Sheriff Hutton is dominated by the gaunt ruins of a 14th-century castle that belonged to the powerful Neville family. Richard Neville, Earl of Warwick, played a major role in the Wars of the Roses, and his daughter married Richard III. This is why the tomb of their son, Edward Prince of Wales, is in the nearby medieval church. He died in 1484 at the age of 11. The picturesque church is of Norman origin but dates mainly from the 13th and 14th centuries.

Start by walking along Main Street, signposted to Parish Church, passing to the left of the castle and church. Where the road ends, keep ahead over a stile – at public footpath Ebor Way and Centenary Way signs – and continue along a track to enter a field. Turn left along its left-hand edge and, at a hedge corner, continue

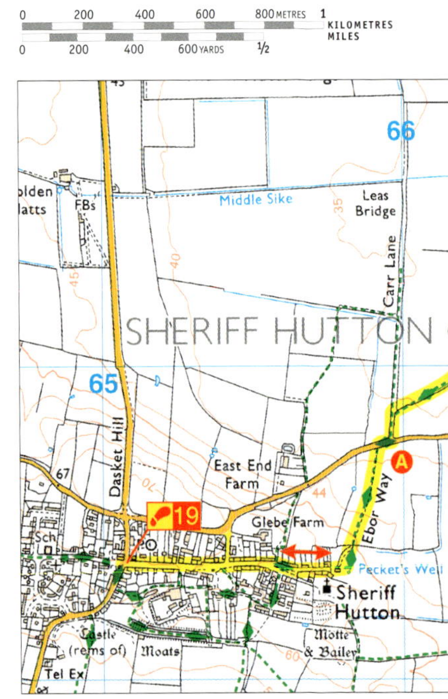

downhill across the field and go through a fence gap onto a road. Turn right and, at a public footpath sign **A**, turn left over a stile and walk along a track. In front of a gate and stile, turn right over another stile and walk along the right-hand edge of a field. Climb a stile, cross a footbridge over a ditch, then cross a gallop and keep ahead along the right-hand edge of the next field. On the far side, bear left **B** along a straight track, cross a bridge over Commission Beck, keep ahead towards Ings Beck. At Ings Beck the definitive

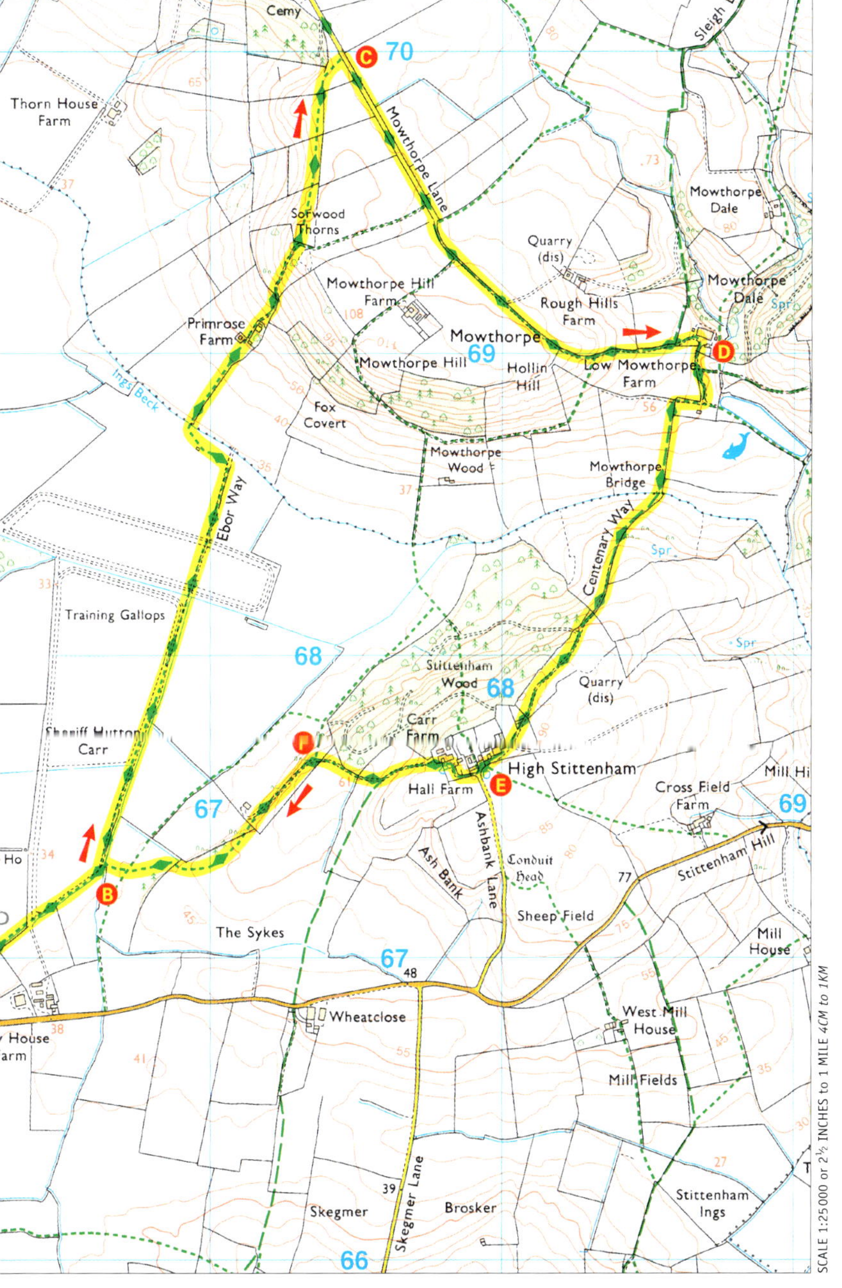

Sheriff Hutton church

path turns left for a few yards just to the south of the beck before crossing a footbridge. (At the time of writing this path was not accessible and after crossing the beck the route skirted the left-hand edge of a field before rejoining the Ebor Way 200 yds [183m] farther on.) Head gently uphill along the right edge of a field towards a farm.

Climb a stile, continue uphill along the right-hand field edge but, before reaching the corner, bear left and head across to a fence corner. Keep ahead, by a fence on the right, passing to the left of the farm, and continue uphill along a track over Mowthorpe Hill to emerge onto a narrow lane **C**. Turn right and, after passing a public bridleway sign, the way continues along a hedge-lined track that descends and bends right in front of Low Mowthorpe Farm **D** to a gate. As you descend, there are superb views ahead looking across the wide expanses of the vale to the line of the Yorkshire Wolds.

Go through the gate, keep ahead along the right-hand edge of a sloping field and, at a waymarked post, turn right alongside a fence on the right.

Climb a stile, turn left to walk along the left-hand edge of the next two fields and, in the corner of the second field, turn first right, then immediately left to cross Mowthorpe Bridge. Go through a gate, continue uphill by a line of trees on the left, go through another gate and keep ahead, following a track over the brow of the hill. To the right is Stittenham Wood. After going through the next gate, walk in front of farm buildings to reach a footpath post at a junction of tracks **E**.

Keep ahead, in the Sheriff Hutton direction, along a tarmac track, which bends right to a T-junction, and turn left through a gate. Keep ahead to go through another gate, and the track descends through a young plantation, curving gradually right to a gate at the bottom. Go through the gate, turn right by the right-hand edge of a field alongside Stittenham Wood but, where the field edge bears slightly right, turn left and head straight across the field to a stile **F**. Climb it, turn left along a narrow path, which gradually descends an embankment, and go through a gate at the bottom. Continue across a low embankment, looking out for a way-marked post by the edge of a field, and keep ahead to the next footpath post.

From here continue straight across the field – the path is likely to be muddy – and on the far side, go through a wide gap and cross a ditch. Turn left **B** along the left-hand edge of the next field, picking up the outward route, and retrace your steps to the start. The houses of Sheriff Hutton, the church tower and the jagged walls of the castle can be seen on the low ridge ahead. ●

Hunmanby, Muston and Stocking Dale

Start	Hunmanby
Distance	7½ miles (12.1km)
Approximate time	3½ hours
Parking	Hunmanby
Refreshments	Pubs and cafés at Hunmanby, pub at Muston
Ordnance Survey maps	Landranger 101 (Scarborough), Explorer 301 (Scarborough, Bridlington & Flamborough Head)

Almost the whole of this attractive and satisfying walk is on the well-waymarked Centenary Way and Wolds Way. Much of it is below the gentle northern slopes of the wolds, not far from the coast, and the many superb views include – near the end – Flamborough Head. The scenic highlight is probably the delightful ramble through the wooded and steep-sided Stocking Dale below Folkton Wold.

The village of Hunmanby lies below the wolds just inland from Filey Bay. Its impressive medieval church dates back to the 12th century and retains much of its Norman architecture.

The walk starts in Cross Hill by the church. Pass to the left of the church and, at a fork, take the right-hand road (Northgate). Where it ends, keep ahead along an enclosed tarmac track, at a

The village of Hunmanby

sign for the Centenary Way. The track later becomes rough. At the gate to North Moor Farm, keep ahead along a short stretch of enclosed path to reach a stile. Climb the stile, walk across a field and then climb another stile on the far side. Continue along another enclosed track, climbing a series of stiles, to eventually emerge onto the A165 at a junction **Ⓐ**.

Turn left – there is a path along the right verge – for a brief stretch along this busy main road and turn left along the A1039 (signposted to Malton) into Muston. Follow the winding road through the village, passing a green, a church and a pub. The church is Victorian, built in 1863 on the site of an earlier one.

Continue beyond the village – *take care as there is no path and not much of a verge* – and at a Wolds Way sign, turn left over a stile **Ⓑ**. Walk along the right-hand edge of a succession of fields, climbing a series of stiles, and finally turn right over a stile in the corner of the last field.

Walk across the next field, making for a footpath post on the far side. Go through a gap in the hedge, turn left along the left-hand edge of fields and pass beside a gate onto a road **Ⓒ**. Cross over, take the track ahead to Stockendale Farm and, on entering a field, bear right along its right-hand edge. To the right are the trees of Long Plantation. After descending into a dip, follow the track to the left, keeping along the bottom edge of a sloping field.

In the corner, keep ahead through trees and on through the steep-sided and well-wooded Stocking Dale, a most attractive part of the walk. Climb a stile, keep ahead and, where the dale opens out at a meeting of dales, continue through Stocking Dale – here leaving the Wolds Way but still following the

Centenary Way – to a stile at a fence corner. Climb it, walk along the left-hand edge of a field to join a track and continue along it, heading uphill and bending left. At a hedge gap on the left – in front of a Private Road notice – turn left along a track **Ⓓ**.

With splendid views over the wolds, follow this undulating track across fields, making for the clump of trees that shelters Field House Farm. Keep

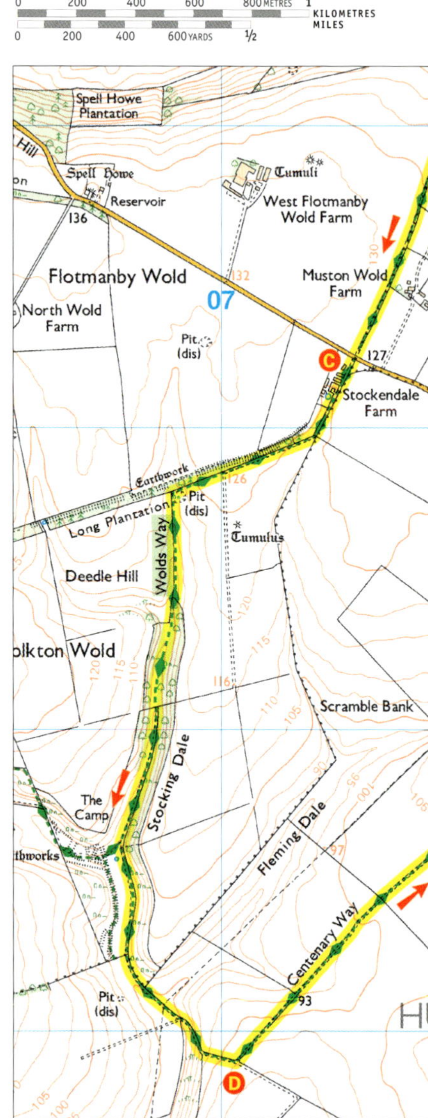

ahead through the trees, turn right along the right-hand edge of a barn, turn left at the corner of the barn and walk along a track, passing to the right of the farmhouse. As you continue walking along a tarmac track,

Flamborough Head can be seen across fields, to the right.

On reaching a road **E**, turn right into Hunmanby and follow the road around a right-hand bend into Church Hill to return to the start.

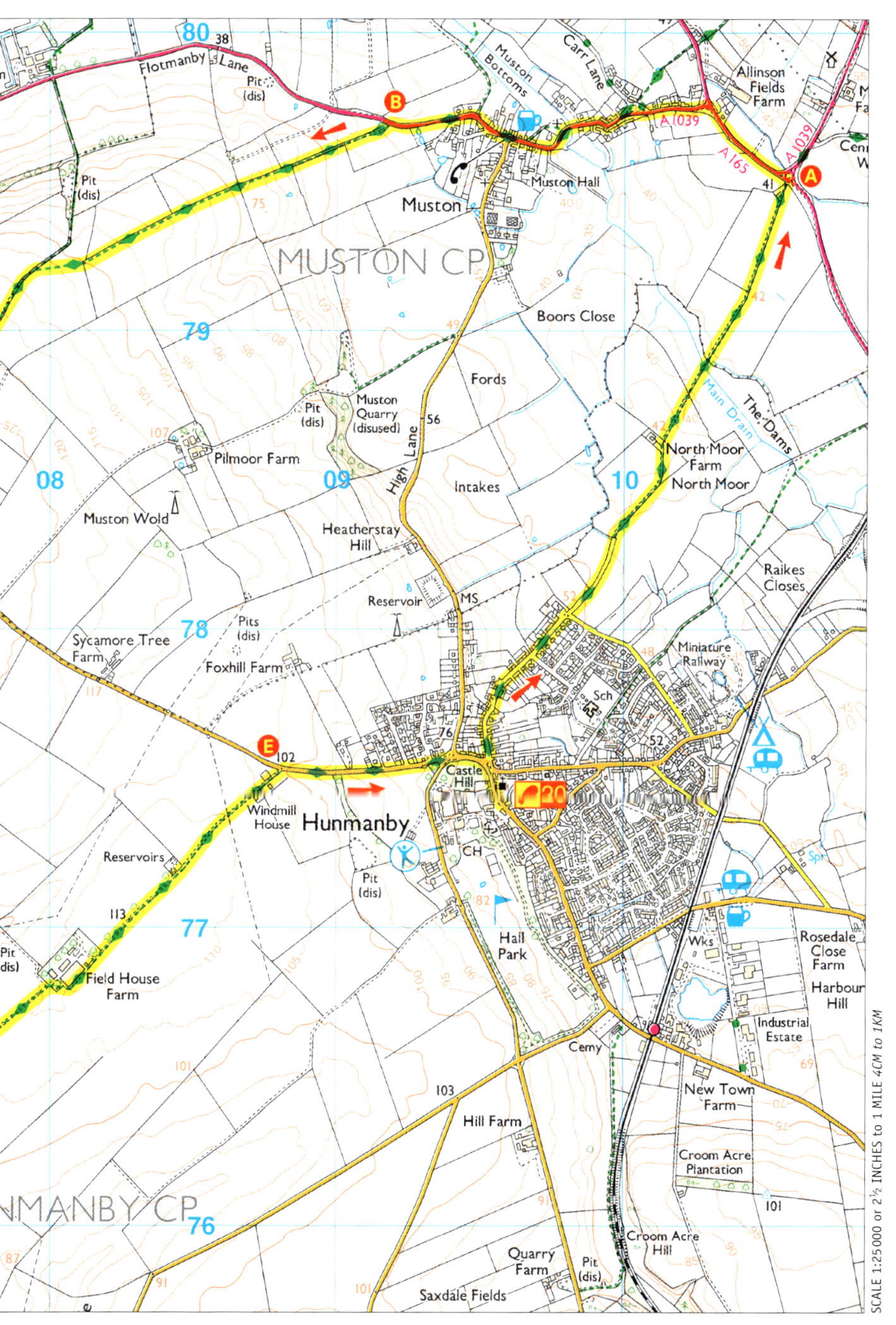

Londesborough Park and Goodmanham

Start	Market Weighton
Distance	7½ miles (12.1km)
Approximate time	3½ hours
Parking	Market Weighton
Refreshments	Pubs and cafés at Market Weighton, pub at Goodmanham
Ordnance Survey maps	Landranger 106 (Market Weighton), Explorer 294 (Market Weighton & Yorkshire Wolds Central)

The whole of this walk is on the Wolds Way, using two alternative routes between Market Weighton and Londesborough Park. Route finding is, therefore, easy. Londesborough Park is a particularly attractive part of the walk, and from there you head across to the village of Goodmanham. A descent into Spring Dale is followed by a final stretch along the track of a disused railway. From many points on the route there are fine and extensive views over the wolds and the Vale of York.

Market Weighton's traditional importance as a route centre increased when it acquired a canal in the 18th century and a railway in the 19th century. Both have gone but the former railway line to Beverley now serves as a public footpath used for the last part of the route. Probably the town's most famous son was William Bradley, the Yorkshire Giant, born here in 1787. He grew to a height of 7ft 9in. (2.36m) and weighed 27 stone (172kg).

The walk begins in the Market Place by the mainly 13th-century church and the Londesborough Arms Hotel, the latter a fine example of a Georgian coaching inn. Facing the hotel and church, turn left and, at a fork, take the right-hand road (York Road). Just beyond the last of the houses, turn right through a kissing-gate **A**, at a public footpath sign to Londesborough Park, and walk across a field. Cross a footbridge over a drain on the far side and continue in a straight line along the right-hand edge of fields to emerge onto a road.

Cross over, take the tree-lined, tarmac drive ahead, pass to the right of a farm and keep ahead to a gate. Go through, walk across a field and, on the far side, pass through a belt of trees and cross a footbridge over Towthorpe Beck. Head across the next field to a gate and stile, climb the stile and continue along the right-hand edge of fields, finally turning right onto a lane **B**. Turn left and, at a Wolds Way sign to Londesborough, turn right between gateposts, here entering Londesborough Park. Pass beside a lodge, climb a stile and keep ahead along a track – the lake can be seen to the right – to a fork **C**.

The route continues along the right-hand track but it is worthwhile making a brief detour along the left-hand track to the church and estate village of Londesborough. The track heads gently uphill to a gate. Go through, continue up through woodland to a crossroads and turn left along a tarmac track to the church **D**.

During its history the Londesborough estate has had a succession of owners, including the earls of Burlington, the Cavendish family (dukes of Devonshire), George Hudson, the 19th-century 'Railway King', and the earls of Londesborough. It was the third Earl of Burlington who landscaped the park, including the lake. The Cavendishes largely neglected it in favour of their main residence at Chatsworth, and the old hall was demolished in 1819. A new one was built in 1839, but on a different site. The earls of Londesborough, who owned the estate from 1850 to 1923, enlarged the new house and restored the parkland. The modest but attractive church has a fine Norman south door. The porch was added in 1679.

Retrace your steps to the fork **C** and turn sharp left, in the Goodmanham direction. Head gently downhill to cross a brook, go through a gate and, at a fork, take the right-hand track, and continue across the parkland to a stile. Climb it, cross a footbridge between two lakes, climb another stile and head uphill, skirting the left-hand corner of woodland and continuing to a stile.

After climbing the stile, turn right along the tarmac track a few yards ahead and, where this track bends right, keep ahead along the right-hand edge of a field to a road **E**.

Goodmanham church

Cross over, take the tarmac drive opposite, but, almost immediately, turn left off it to continue along a track across fields. The track bends left and, as you head downhill along the right-hand edge of fields, the houses of Goodmanham can be seen ahead sheltering below the wolds. Later, you curve right along an enclosed track to pass under a disused railway bridge and head uphill. Take the left-hand path, continuing up to emerge onto a road in the village, and keep ahead to a T-junction by the church **F**.

It is difficult to believe that this sleepy village was once the site of a pagan temple, possibly under the mainly Norman church. At the T-junction, turn right for the pub but the route continues uphill to the left. Turn right, at a Wolds Way sign, along a narrow lane – the tower of Market Weighton church can be seen over to the right – and the lane descends between hedgebanks, bends left and continues down into the dale. Where the lane curves right, turn right through a fence gap to join the Hudson Way **G**, a footpath that uses the track of the disused Market Weighton to Beverley railway line, which was opened in 1865 and closed down exactly a century later.

Follow the straight path, which is lined with hedges and trees, through Spring Dale back to Market Weighton, a distance of about 1$\frac{1}{2}$ miles (2.4km). The path eventually reaches a road on the edge of the town. Do not continue along it but bear left across a grassy area to a track and bear left again – the track shortly becomes a road – to the church. Pass to the left of the church to return to the starting point of the walk in the town.

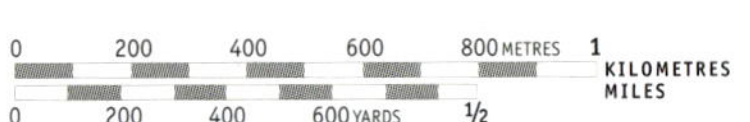

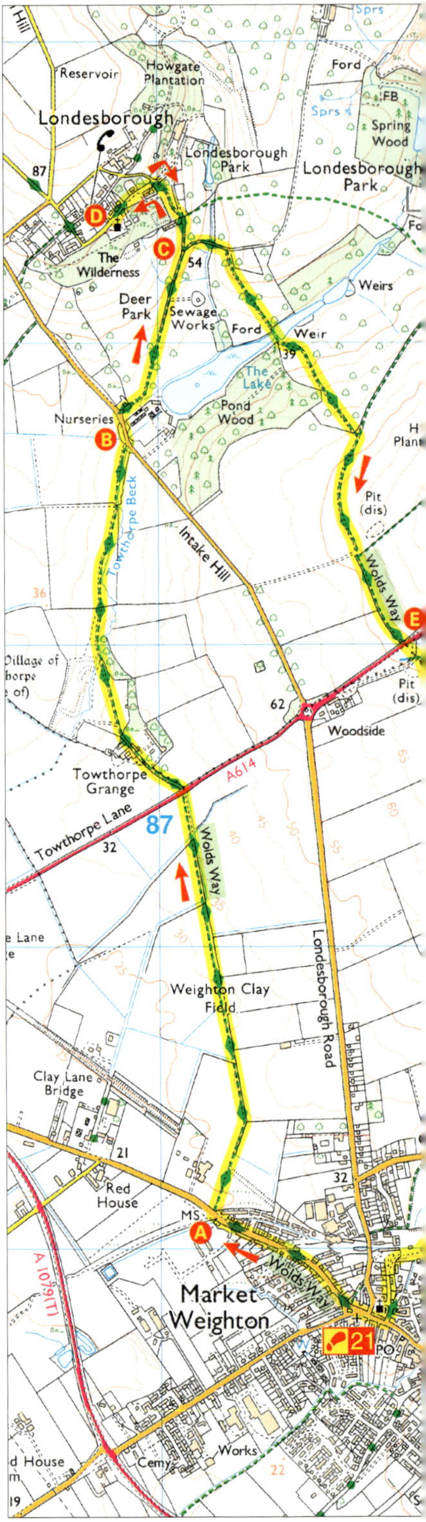

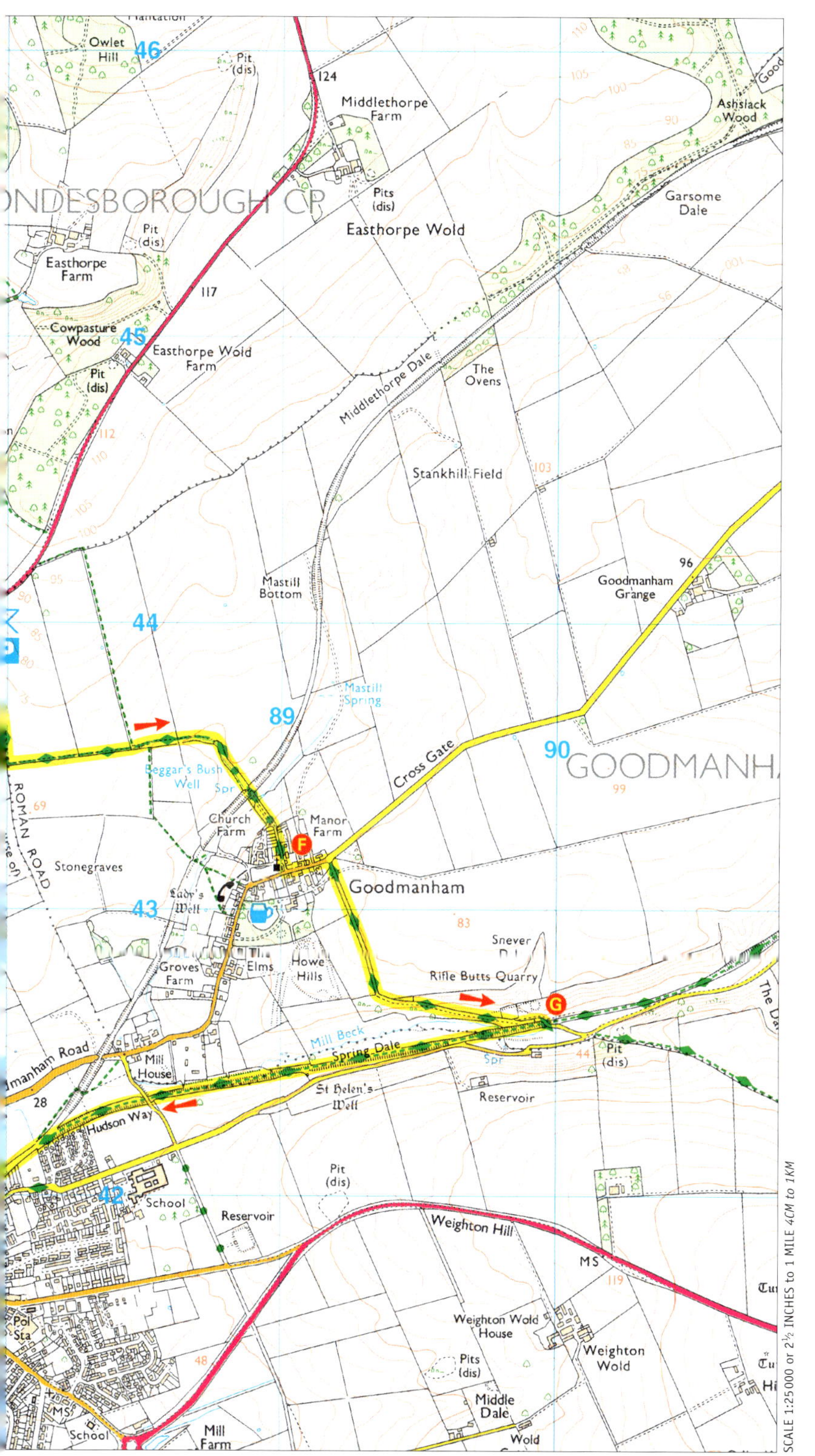

Owlet Hill
46
Plantation
Pit (dis)
124
Middlethorpe Farm
Ashslack Wood
Garsome Dale
LONDESBOROUGH CP
Pit (dis)
Easthorpe Wold
Pits (dis)
Easthorpe Farm
117
45
Easthorpe Wold Farm
Pit (dis)
Cowpasture Wood
Middlethorpe Dale
The Ovens
Stankhill Field
103
112
Mastill Bottom
Goodmanham Grange
96
44
Mastill Spring
89
Beggar's Bush Well
Spr
Cross Gate
90
GOODMANH
99
ROMAN ROAD
Church Farm
Manor Farm
F
Stonegraves
Goodmanham
Lady's Well
43
Snever
83
Groves Farm
Elms
Howe Hills
Rifle Butts Quarry
G
The Da
Mill Beck
Spring Dale
Spr
44
Pit (dis)
manham Road
Mill House
St Helen's Well
Reservoir
28
Hudson Way
Pit (dis)
42
School
Reservoir
Weighton Hill
MS
119
Pol Sta
48
Weighton Wold House
Weighton Wold
Tu
MS
Middle Dale
School
Mill Farm
Wold
SCALE 1:25000 or 2½ INCHES to 1 MILE 4CM to 1KM

Tadcaster and Healaugh

Start	Tadcaster, at north end of the bridge over the River Wharfe
Distance	8 miles (12.9km)
Approximate time	4 hours
Parking	Tadcaster
Refreshments	Pubs and cafés at Tadcaster
Ordnance Survey maps	Landranger 105 (York & Selby), Explorer 290 (York)

After a short opening stretch beside the River Wharfe, almost the whole of the walk is on tracks and field paths. It takes you across the pleasant and gently undulating countryside of the Vale of York lying to the north of the Wharfe valley between York and Tadcaster. At the half-way point it passes through the quiet village of Healaugh. Route finding on parts of the return leg are somewhat tortuous at times so the directions need to be followed carefully.

The skyline of Tadcaster is dominated by the various breweries for which the town is famous. It grew up as a crossing place on the River Wharfe and was once an important river port. The impressive, mainly 15th-century church lies by the river but because it was being damaged by frequent flooding the entire building – apart from the tower – was dismantled in 1875 and re-erected on new, higher foundations.

Start at the north end of the 18th-century bridge over the Wharfe, cross it and, at a public footpath sign to Newton Kyme, turn sharp right along a tarmac path beside the river. After passing to the right of the church, turn left **A** alongside the low churchyard wall to a road, turn sharp right, bear right at the war memorial and turn right along the road signposted to Boston Spa and Wetherby.

Opposite the Bass Brewery, turn right through a fence gap **B**, walk along a tree-lined path and cross a viaduct. The viaduct was constructed to carry a railway line over the Wharfe valley but was not used as the railway was never built. On the other side, turn sharp right down steps and, at the bottom, turn right to pass under the viaduct. Continue beside the river but, before reaching the corner of the field, bear right away from it gently uphill to a waymarked stile. Climb it, continue diagonally uphill across the next field and, in the far corner, climb two stiles in quick succession onto a road. Turn right and, after approximately ¼ mile (400m), turn left **C** at a public bridleway sign, along a track. The track bends left, passes to the left of Broadfield Farm and, shortly after a right bend, reaches a crossroads **D**.

Turn left at a public bridleway sign to

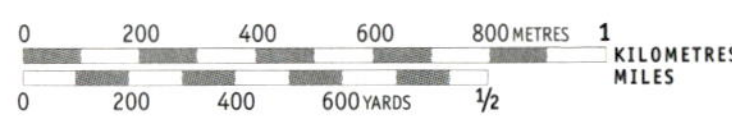

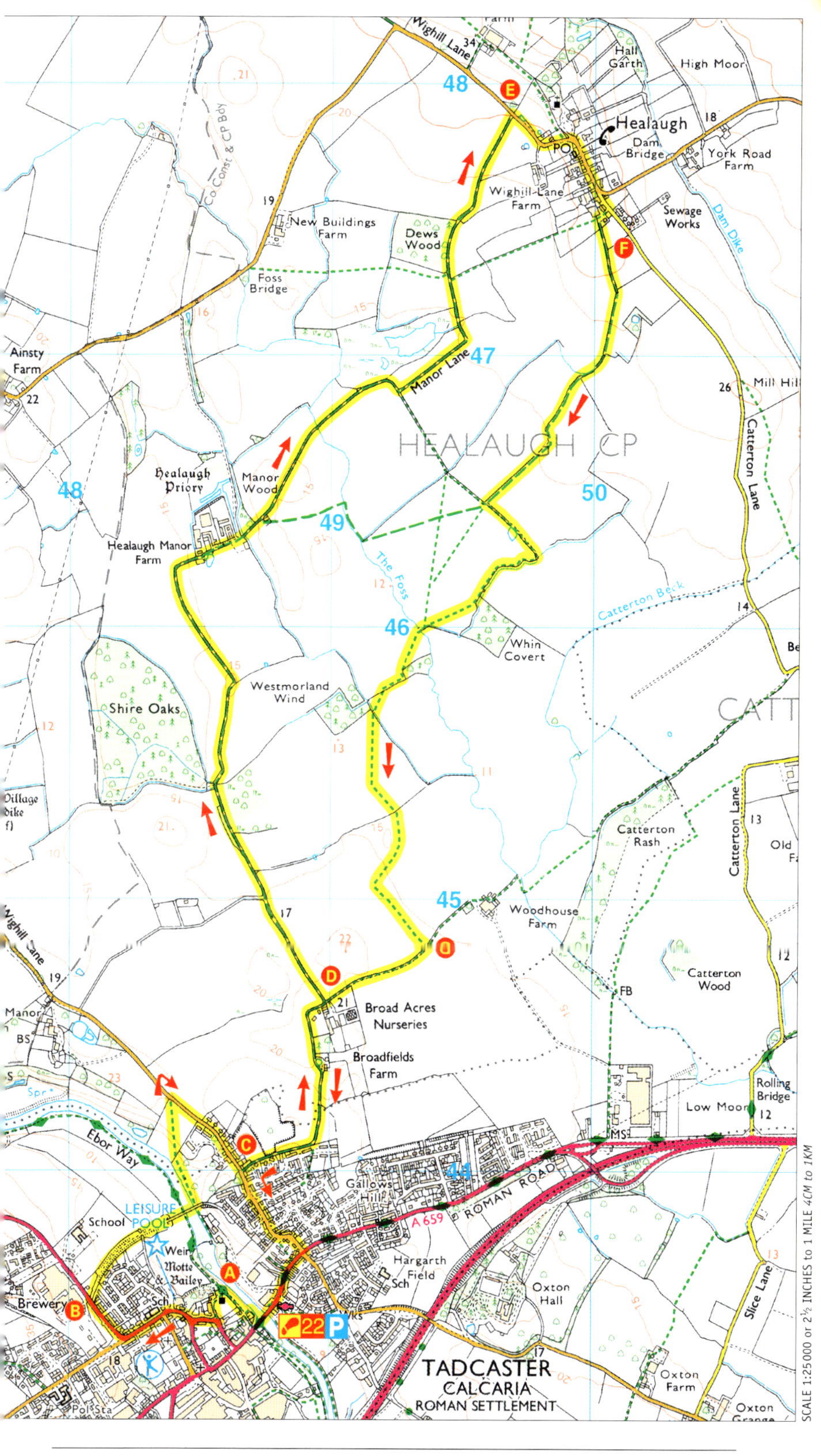

Wighill Lane
Farm
34
PO
Hall Garth
High Moor
48
E
Healaugh
18
Wighill Lane Farm
PO
Dam Bridge
York Road Farm
F
Sewage Works
Dam Dike
New Buildings Farm
Dews Wood
19
Foss Bridge
16
Manor Lane
47
HEALAUGH CP
26
Mill Hill
Ainsty Farm
22
Healaugh Priory
Manor Wood
Catterton Lane
Healaugh Manor Farm
48
49
50
The Foss
12
Catterton Beck
14
46
Whin Covert
CATT
Shire Oaks
Westmorland Wind
13
Dillage dike (f)
21
15
11
45
Catterton Rash
13
Old Fa
17
Woodhouse Farm
Catterton Wood
12
Wighill Lane
19
22
D
C
Manor
BS
S
23
Spr
21
Broad Acres Nurseries
Broadfields Farm
FB
Low Moor
12
Rolling Bridge
MS
Ebor Way
C
Gallows Hill
44
ROMAN ROAD
A 659
Slice Lane
13
LEISURE POOL
School
Weir
Motte & Bailey
A
Hargarth Field
Hargarth Sch
Oxton Hall
Brewery
B
Sch
22
P
Oxton Farm
17
TADCASTER
CALCARIA
ROMAN SETTLEMENT
Pol Sta
18
Oxton Grange
SCALE 1:25 000 or 2½ INCHES to 1 MILE 4CM to 1KM

Tadcaster church

Healaugh and follow a winding, hedge-lined track for just over one mile (1.6km), finally bending right to Healaugh Manor Farm. The farm, built on the site of the vanished Healaugh Priory, has something of a monastic appearance. Passing to the right of the farm buildings, keep ahead along a track, following it around a right-hand bend to a junction of tracks. Turn left to continue along the main track – there are views of Healaugh Church on a slight rise above the village – which emerges onto a road and turn right **E** into Healaugh. The church is predominantly Norman, with a short conical spire on the 12th-century tower and a superb south doorway.

Where the road turns left, keep ahead along a lane signposted to Catterton and, at a public bridleway sign, turn right **F** through a gate into a farmyard. Turn left along a winding track, go through two gates in quick succession and keep ahead to the next gate, where the track ends. So far, route finding could hardly have been more straightforward but from now on it becomes more complex.

After going through the gate, keep ahead across a field, go through a gate on the far side, walk along a short stretch of enclosed track and go through another gate to a T-junction. Turn left along a hedge-lined track and, in front of a gate, turn right – there is a yellow waymark here – to go through another gate.

Keep along the left-hand edge of a field – which follows the meanders of a brook on the other side of the hedge – and look out for a yellow waymark at the corner of a wood. This directs you to bear right and head diagonally across the field to a stile in the far corner.

Climb the stile, cross a footbridge over a brook, bear slightly left across the corner of the next field to the corner of trees and bear left along the left-hand field edge. In the corner, turn right to continue along the left-hand edge of the field and look out for a waymarked post where you bear left through a hedge gap. Head diagonally across a field corner to the next waymarked post, keep ahead through a hedge gap and walk diagonally across the next field, veering left to go through another hedge gap. There is no waymark here and the precise spot is not particularly clear but it is about 200 yds (183m) from the left corner of the field and in line with three trees in the next field.

After passing through the gap, make for those three trees – the first is waymarked – and at the third tree, bear right across to a solitary tree (also waymarked). From here, bear slightly right again and continue across the field to a hedge. Turn left alongside the hedge to a track and turn right **G**. At a crossroads keep ahead **D**, here rejoining the outward route, and retrace your steps to the road **C**.

For a more direct return to the start, turn left and at traffic lights turn right downhill back into the centre of Tadcaster.

Hornsea Mere and the Rail Trail

Start	Hornsea, corner of Marine Drive and New Road
Distance	8½ miles (13.7km)
Approximate time	4 hours
Parking	Hornsea
Refreshments	Pubs and cafés at Hornsea
Ordnance Survey maps	Landranger 107 (Kingston upon Hull), Explorer 295 (Bridlington, Driffield & Hornsea)

From the seafront at Hornsea, the route first heads through the town centre and then across meadows beside Hornsea Mere, the largest lake in Yorkshire. It continues across fields, through woods and along lanes, and the final 2½ miles (4km) is along the Hornsea Rail Trail, a disused railway track. There are pleasant wooded stretches and wide views across the mere and over the surrounding flat countryside of Holderness.

The walk begins on the seafront at the point where Marine Drive turns away from the sea to become New Road. Walk along New Road and, at a junction, bear left along Newbegin into the town centre.

With its fine sandy beach, Hornsea developed into a seaside resort in the 19th century, especially after the coming of the railway, and the promenade is typically Victorian. But in the town centre, ½ mile (800m) inland, there is an older Hornsea, with some attractive old cottages and an impressive medieval church.

At a T-junction by the church **A**, turn left, turn right along Hull Road and, at a public footpath sign 'Hornsea Mere Walk', turn right through a kissing-gate **B**. Walk across a meadow bordering Hornsea Mere – waymarked posts indicate the line of the route – go through a kissing-gate and continue along the left-hand edge of a succession of meadows, passing through several hedge gaps, to reach a kissing-gate. Go through and keep straight ahead across the next two fields, going through another kissing-gate. On the far side of the second field, go through two kissing-gates in quick succession and

Hornsea Rail Trail

over the intervening plank footbridge.

Bear slightly left across the next field and, in the corner, go through a kissing-gate onto a track. Turn right through a gate, walk along the track, climb a stile and keep ahead – at a public bridleway sign – initially between trees and then across a field. To the left the façade of Wassand Hall can be seen. Go through a gate in the field corner, keep ahead along a tree-lined track – it soon becomes a tarmac one – take the first track on the left but almost immediately

bear right, at a public footpath sign, to continue along a path through trees to reach a stile. After climbing the stile, continue across a field and, just beyond the second waymarked post, turn left along a track **C**.

Go through a gate, continue along the tree-lined track to a narrow lane, keep ahead along it and, after ½ mile (800m), turn left through a gate **D** at a public bridleway sign. Walk along the right-hand edge of a field towards a farm, go through a gate, keep ahead along a fence-lined track and, just before it bends left, go through a gate on the right. Keep ahead to go through another gate and join a tarmac drive, passing to the right of the farmhouse. Turn right and continue along the drive to rejoin the narrow lane **E**. Turn left and, after about $1\frac{1}{4}$ miles (2km), turn left through a fence gap, at a public footpath sign, to join the Hornsea Rail Trail **F**. This footpath and cycleway uses the former Hull to Hornsea railway line, which opened in 1864 and closed just over a century later.

Keep along this pleasant, tree- and hedge-lined track to the edge of the town and pass beside a gate onto a tarmac track. Here there is a break in the former railway track and, to rejoin it, turn right to a road, turn sharp left and, at a junction, keep ahead up steps. There is a public footpath sign here. Continue along the top of a tree-lined embankment, finally emerging on to a road by the restored former railway station building. Turn right towards the sea and the turn left along the promenade to return to the starting point of the walk.

Hornsea Mere

Nether Poppleton and the River Ouse

Start	Nether Poppleton
Distance	9 miles (14.5km)
Approximate time	4½ hours
Parking	Roadside parking at Nether Poppleton
Refreshments	Pub at Nether Poppleton
Ordnance Survey maps	Landranger 105 (York & Selby), Explorer 290 (York)

The first half of this lengthy though easy walk in the flat countryside just to the west of York is across fields to reach the banks of the River Nidd near Moor Monkton. The Nidd is followed for a short distance to its confluence with the Ouse, and the remainder of the route – over 3½ miles (5.6km) – is across meadows bordering the Ouse. The additional short loop around Nether Poppleton is worthwhile for the chance to see the small Norman church and restored tithe barn and for the distant view of the towers of York Minster.

Start at the junction of roads in the village centre and turn along Main Street. Ignore two public bridleway signs on the right but, at a public footpath sign, turn right over a stile Ⓐ and follow a path across fields. Approaching a farm, keep to the left of a hedge, pass between gateposts and continue along a track, passing to the right of the farm buildings.

Where the track turns left at the corner of a barn, turn right to enter a field and turn left along its left-hand edge, above a ditch. In the field corner turn right to continue along the left-hand field edge, go through a hedge gap and keep along the edge of the next field to a T-junction Ⓑ. Turn right along a track and, after a long, straight section, the track bends left in front of a building. Where the track bends right, keep ahead over a stile and walk across a field to climb another stile on the far side.

Cross a ditch, keep along the right-hand edge of a field to a track and turn right, not along the track but through a gate just beyond it. Walk along the right-hand field edge, turn left in the corner to continue along the edge towards the next farm, go through a gate and keep ahead to join a tarmac track. Pass to the left of the farmhouse, follow this winding track and go through a gate onto a lane. Go through the gate opposite, at a public bridleway sign, and keep first by a garden fence on the left and then along the right-hand edge of a field.

In the field corner, turn left to continue by its right edge, go through a gate, keep along the right edge of the next field above a ditch and follow the ditch around a right-hand bend Ⓒ.

Keep ahead to go through a gate and continue along a hedge-lined path to enter a field. Now keep along the left-hand edge of a succession of fields, going through a series of gates, eventually emerging onto a track. Walk along it, passing to the right of houses, and the track becomes a lane.

Where the lane curves left into Moor Monkton, turn right **D** through a double gate and walk along the track to Launds House Farm. The River Nidd is over to the left. Where the track bends right, keep straight ahead along a grassy path and bear slightly left to descend an embankment to a gate. Go through the gate – and another one – and walk across a field to a footpath post by the confluence of the Nidd and the Ouse **E**. On the opposite bank of the river is a fine view of the houses and church at Nun Monkton. The latter comprises the nave of a Benedictine priory founded in 1153. Turn right to follow the Ouse to Nether Poppleton.

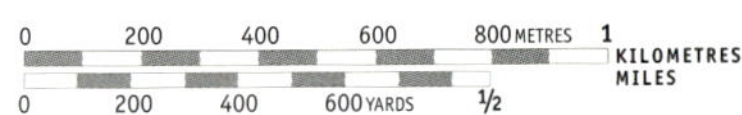

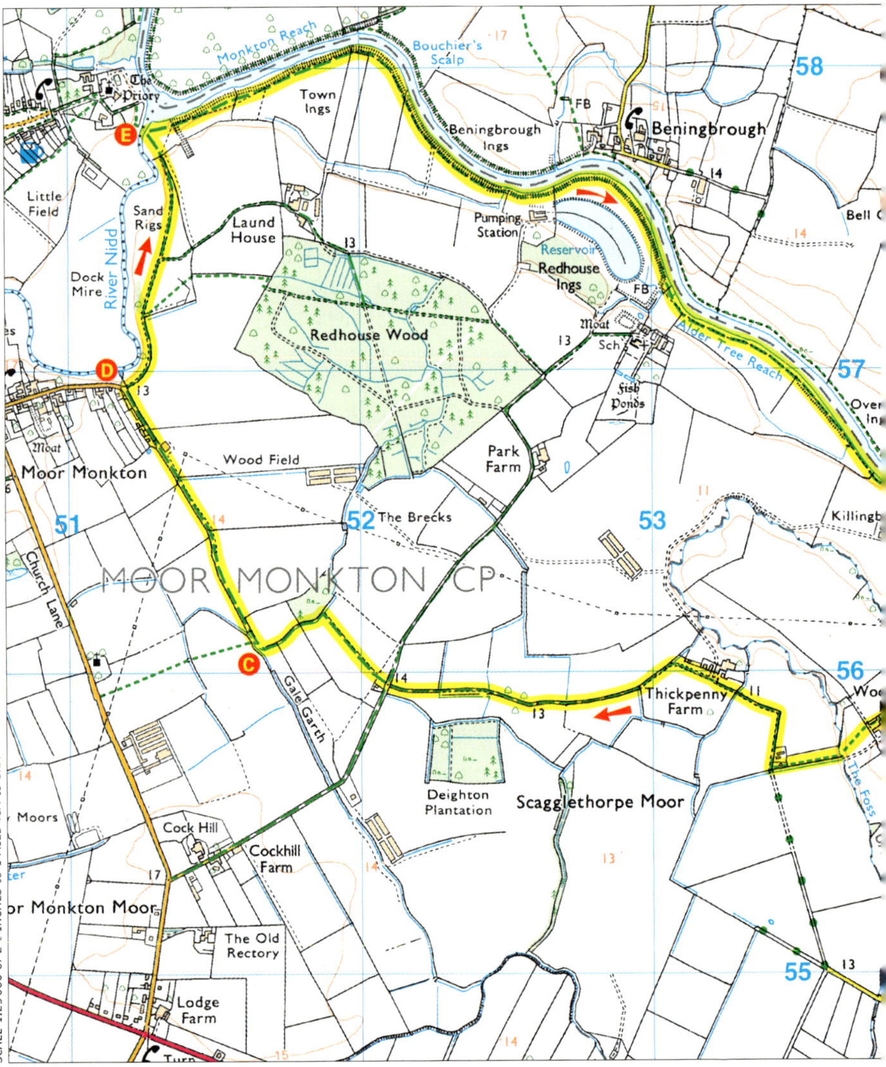

SCALE 1:25 000 or 2½ INCHES to 1 MILE 4CM to 1KM

Most of the route is across meadows beside the river – negotiating a succession of stiles and gates – but at one point you bear slightly right away from the river alongside a stream. Two gates and a footbridge over the stream return you to the riverside path. Finally, on approaching Nether Poppleton, bear left off a track to cross a footbridge, continue by the river up to a road and bear left to return to the start.

For the short extra loop around Nether Poppleton, walk along Church Lane, which curves right to the tithe barn and church. The delightful 12th-century church, one of only two in the country dedicated to St Everilda, a little-known Saxon lady, has a superb Norman chancel arch. The tithe barn, recently restored, dates from the early 16th century, although the brickwork was added about 200 years later.

Opposite the barn and at a public footpath sign to Millfield Lane, turn sharp right through a kissing-gate **F**. Walk along an enclosed path, go

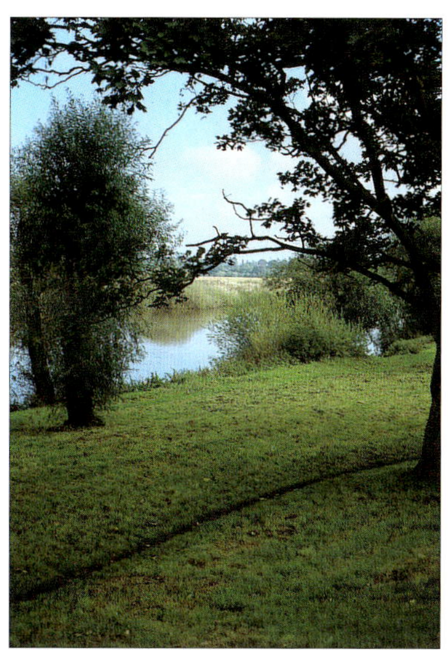

River Ouse near Nether Poppleton

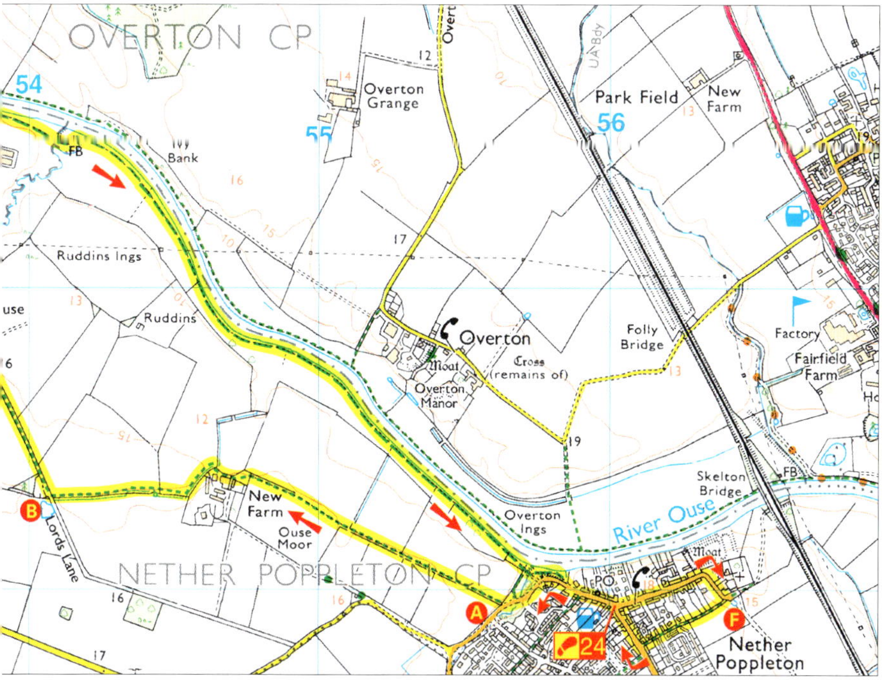

through a gate and keep ahead to a road. Across the fields to the left the towers of York Minster can be seen. Cross the road, keep ahead along an enclosed path to the next road and turn right to the start.

Welton Dale and Brantingham Wold

Start	Welton
Distance	8½ miles (13.7km)
Approximate time	4 hours
Parking	Some parking spaces around the Green at Welton in front of the Green Dragon
Refreshments	Pub at Welton, pub and light refreshments at the post office at Brantingham
Ordnance Survey maps	Landranger 106 (Market Weighton), Explorer 293 (Kingston upon Hull & Beverley)

This walk on the southern edge of the Yorkshire Wolds takes you through a classic wolds landscape of narrow wooded valleys and rolling open uplands. It includes two outstandingly attractive villages, both with pubs and fine churches, and some splendid wooded stretches. From the higher and more open parts of the route, the views extend across the wolds to the Vale of York, the River Humber and Hull. None of the ascents and descents is steep or strenuous.

Welton has all the ingredients of the traditional English village: old cottages, duck pond, pub and church grouped around a green. The sturdy-looking, cruciform church is of medieval origins but underwent a major restoration in the 1860s. Welton's main claim to fame is that it was here that Dick Turpin was arrested in 1739, apparently as a result of getting drunk in the Green Dragon.

Start at The Green and, with your back to the Green Dragon, walk along Cowgate, passing to the left of the church and pond. Keep ahead at a crossroads along Dale Road, passing to the left of a triangular green. Where the road ends, continue along the track through Welton Dale. Keep ahead through the well-wooded dale, gradually ascending all the while and going through three kissing-gates.

After the third gate – which is at the head of the dale and the far end of the woodland – cross a track, climb the stile opposite and turn left **A** along the left-hand edge of a field to a road. Turn left gently downhill and, at a public footpath sign, turn right through a kissing-gate **B** and walk along a path through trees. Descend to a crossing of paths, keep ahead in the Brantingham direction, and the path winds downhill through the wood to go through a kissing-gate onto a lane. Go through the kissing-gate opposite and continue along a wooded path, which heads uphill to a T-junction. Turn right and, in front of a metal gate, turn left through a fence gap, ascend steps, continue through the trees and go through a

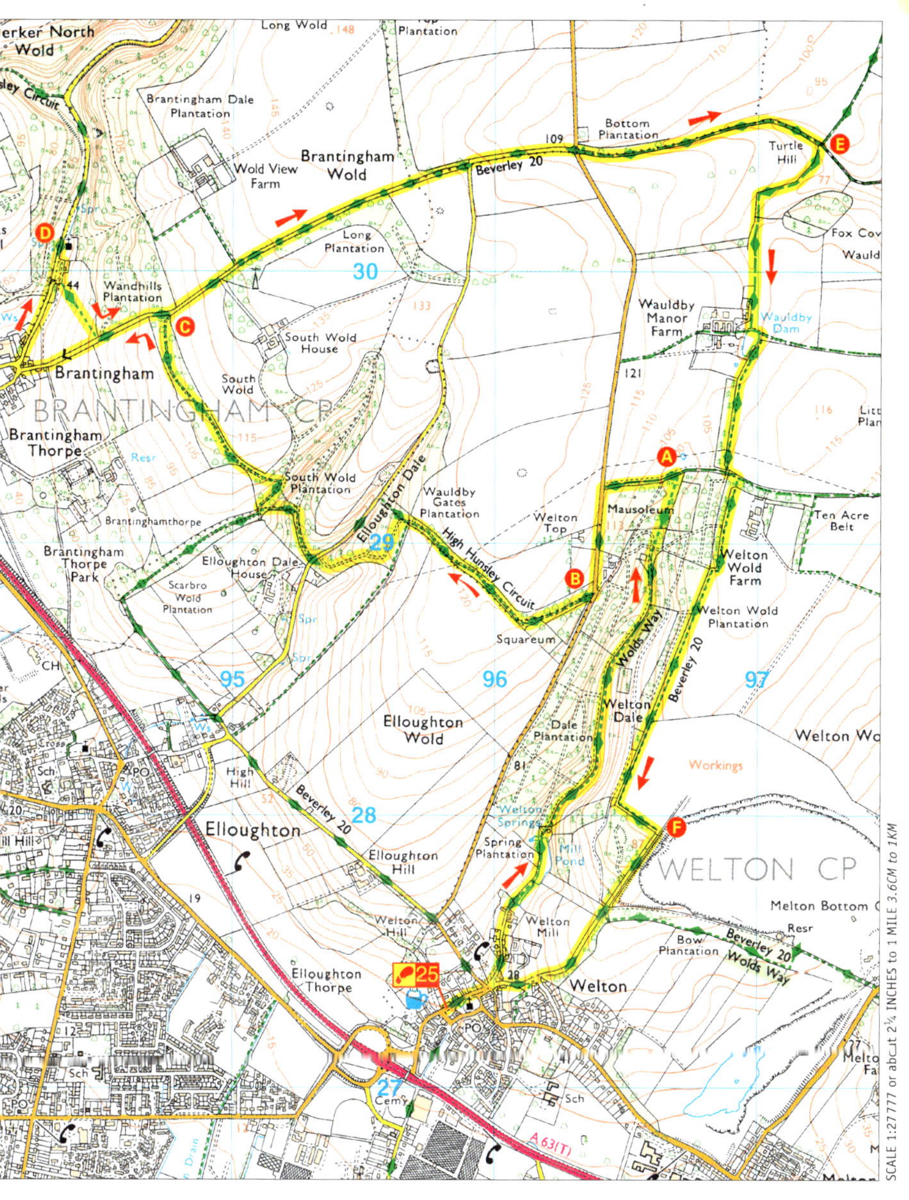

kissing-gate onto a tarmac track **C**.

The route continues to the right but a short detour to the left downhill into Brantingham village and on to the church is thoroughly recommended. On reaching the village, keep ahead for the pub and post office café; otherwise take the first lane on the right, which brings you to the picturesque church **D**. This was mainly rebuilt in 1872, except for the west tower, and is particularly noted for its beautiful location at the foot of wooded Brantingham Dale.

Before reaching the church, turn right onto a track and turn right again across grass to a stile. Climb it, follow a grassy path uphill and climb another stile to rejoin the tarmac track. Turn left uphill, and the track becomes a broad rough track that continues across Brantingham Wold to a lane. Keep ahead to a T-junction, where you continue along a tree-lined path to a crossing of paths and tracks **E**. Turn right along a track, follow it around a left-hand bend and continue to a T-junction to the left of a farm.

Turn left and, at a Wolds Way fingerpost, turn right along the right-hand edge of a field. The way continues alongside trees on the right and, in the field corner, keep ahead into woodland to a T-junction. Turn left and, at a waymarked post a few yards ahead, turn right over a stile, cross a track and keep ahead along a path, initially through trees and later along a right-hand field edge. To the right are the woodlands of Welton Dale, passed through near the start of the walk, and over to the left the Humber Bridge can be seen.

In the field corner, keep ahead along an enclosed path which bends left to a kissing-gate. Go through and turn right along a tree-lined track **F**. The track heads gently downhill into Welton and, on the edge of the village, continue down Chapel Hill back to the start.

Welton

Beverley

Start	Beverley, Market Cross
Distance	9 miles (14.5km)
Approximate time	4½ hours
Parking	Beverley
Refreshments	Pubs and cafés at Beverley
Ordnance Survey maps	Landrangers 106 (Market Weighton) and 107 (Kingston upon Hull), Explorer 293 (Kingston upon Hull & Beverley)

The walk explores the gently undulating countryside to the south and west of Beverley on the edge of the wolds. Beverley Minster inevitably figures prominently in the many wide views which, in places, extend to the Humber and the tower blocks of Hull. The views are particularly outstanding on the final stretch across the open common land of the Westwood. Although lengthy, this is an undemanding walk but be prepared for some muddy paths at times. Allow plenty of time for a thorough exploration of Beverley, an outstandingly attractive and interesting town.

The historic town of Beverley, traditional capital of the East Riding of Yorkshire, has not one but two magnificent medieval churches, the minster to the south of the town centre and St Mary's to the north. Between them is a maze of narrow streets lined by fine old buildings, some of them Georgian, which are explored at the start of the walk.

The tall western towers of Beverley Minster rise above meadows on the south side of the town. Founded in the 7th century by St John of Beverley, the present church dates mainly from the 13th and 14th centuries. It was a collegiate church of the archbishops of York and, with its lofty nave, double transepts and magnificent west front, it is regarded as one of the finest Gothic structures in Europe. Entry is by the ornate 15th-century north porch.

Almost as grand is the cruciform St Mary's Church, built in the 14th and 15th centuries, a superb example of a town church and a reflection of Beverley's prosperity at the time. Nearby is the one surviving gateway of the town's medieval defences, the 15th-century, brick-built North Bar. Close to the minster the remains of a medieval friary have been converted into a youth hostel.

Start at the 18th-century Market Cross in Saturday Market and turn down the Gavel. At a fork, take the left-hand street to reach Wednesday Market and continue along Highgate towards the minster. Turn right at a T-junction in front of the minster, turn left along St John Street, cross a road and keep ahead along Long Lane. Follow the lane around a right-hand bend and, at a public footpath sign 'Beverley Beaver

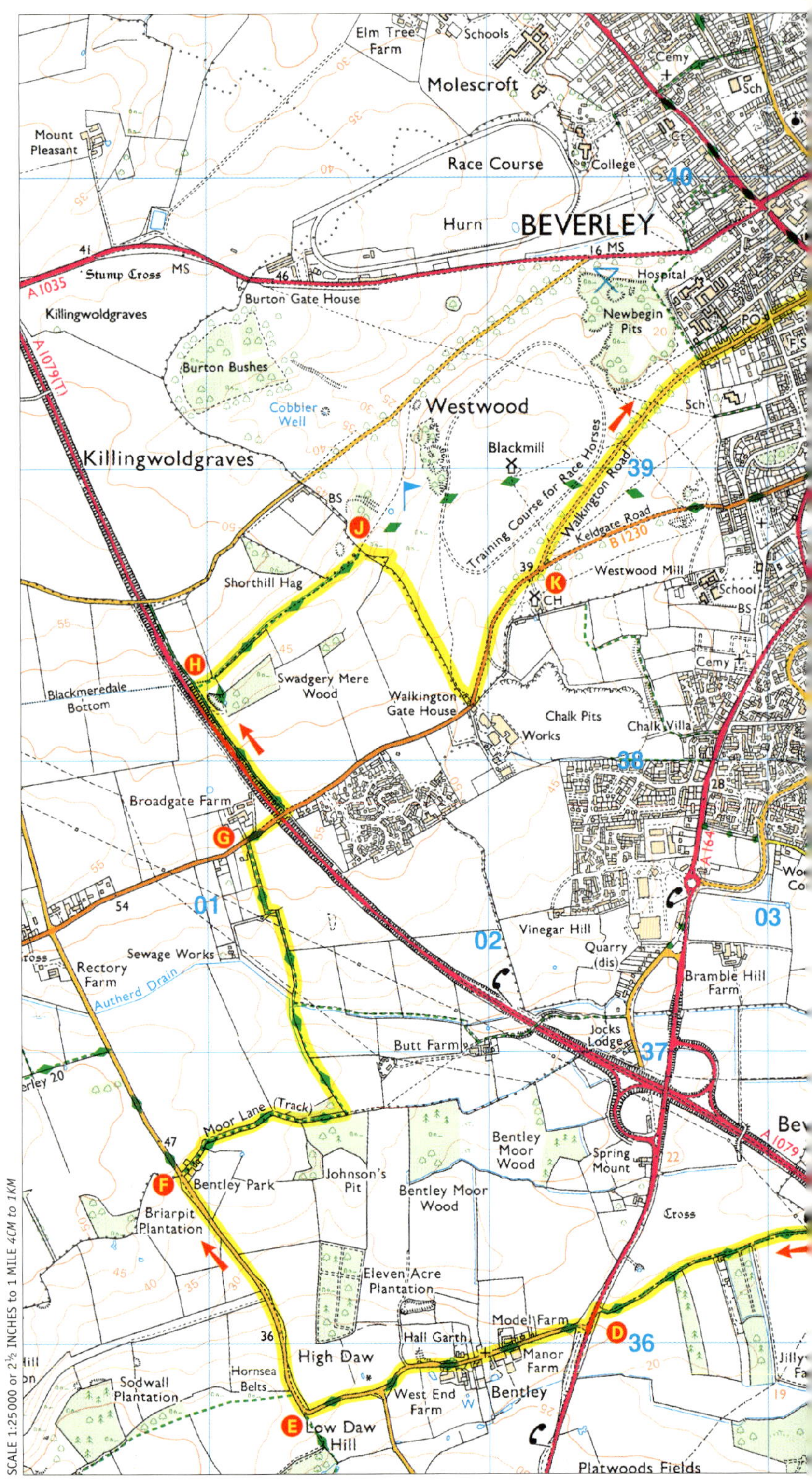

Mount Pleasant
Elm Tree Farm
Schools
Molescroft
Cemy
Sch
Gt
College
Race Course
Hurn
BEVERLEY
16 MS
Hospital
A 1035
Stump Cross
MS
46
Newbegin Pits
Killingwoldgraves
Burton Gate House
A 1079(T)
Burton Bushes
Cobbler Well
Westwood
Sch
Blackmill
Killingwoldgraves
Walkington Road
39
Training Course for Race Horses
Keldgate Road
B1230
BS
J
Westwood Mill
School
BS
39
Shorthill Hag
CH
K
Cemy
H
Swadgery Mere Wood
Walkington Gate House
Chalk Pits
Chalk Villa
Blackmeredale Bottom
45
Works
38
Broadgate Farm
28
A 164
G
54
01
02
Vinegar Hill
Quarry (dis)
03
Woo Co
Sewage Works
Rectory Farm
Bramble Hill Farm
Autherd Drain
Butt Farm
Jocks Lodge
37
Moor Lane (Track)
Bentley Moor Wood
Spring Mount
22
Bev
A 1079
47
Johnson's Pit
Bentley Moor Wood
F
Bentley Park
Briarpit Plantation
Cross
45
Eleven Acre Plantation
40
35
Model Farm
D
36
36
Hall Garth
Manor Farm
Jilly Fa
High Daw
Sodwall Plantation
Hornsea Belts
West End Farm
Bentley
19
E
Low Daw Hill
Platwoods Fields
SCALE 1:25000 or 2½ INCHES to 1 MILE 4CM to 1KM

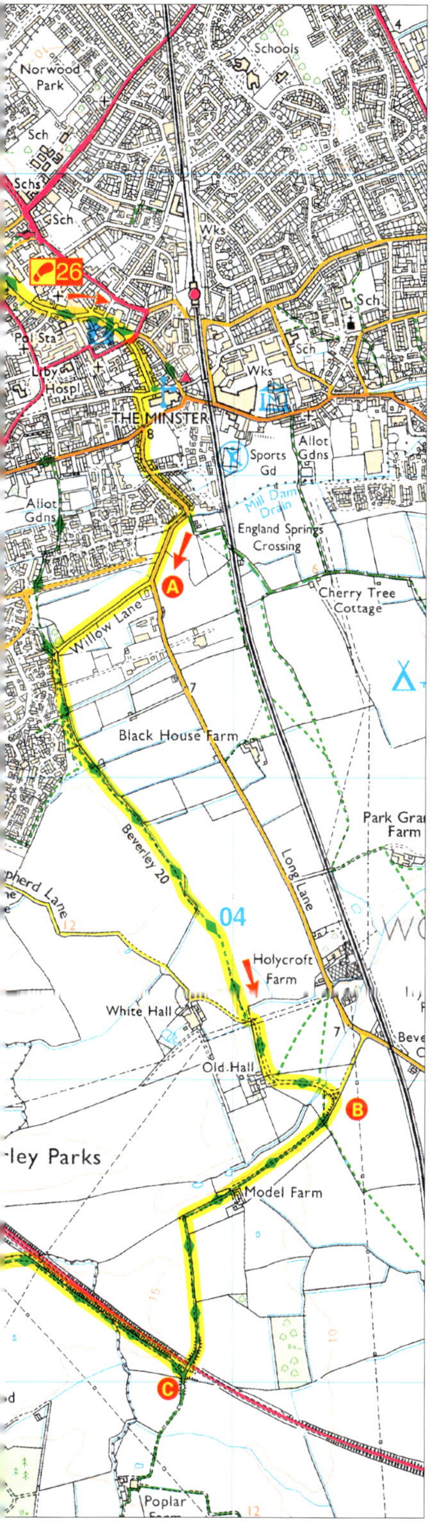

Trail', turn right **A** along a hedge-lined track. Climb a stile, keep ahead, climb another stile to a T-junction and turn left along a winding tarmac path that borders gardens on the right.

At a T-junction, turn left along another tarmac path and, at the next T-junction, turn left again and cross a footbridge over a drain. Walk along the left-hand edge of a field, following the curves of the drain, and cross a footbridge over it where it bends right. Keep ahead across the next field to emerge onto a lane, turn left and immediately follow the lane around a right-hand bend. The lane bends left by a farm and, where it bends left again, turn right along a farm track **B**. After passing to the right of the farm, the track turns left and crosses a bridge over a main road. On the other side, turn right **C** along a track parallel to the road and continue along the right edge of fields, gradually curving left to emerge onto a tarmac track.

Keep ahead to a road **D**, cross over, bear left along a tarmac path to join a lane and follow it through Bentley. On meeting a road, continue along it, follow it around a right-hand bend **E** and after about ½ mile (800m) – just before the brow of a low hill and at a public footpath sign Beverley 20 – turn right along a track **F**.

You follow the regular Beverley 20 signs for much of the rest of the route. Keep along the hedge-lined track to the next footpath sign and turn left onto an enclosed path. Turn left to cross a footbridge over a drain, go through a kissing-gate and walk along the left-hand edge of the next two fields, going through another kissing-gate and heading down to cross a footbridge in a dip.

Keep along the left-hand edge of the

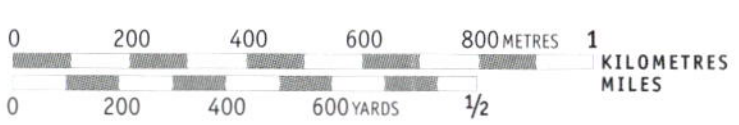

next field, climb a stile in the corner and continue along a tree-lined path. Turn left at a public footpath sign and, at a T-junction, turn right along an enclosed track, climb a stile and continue to a road **G**. Turn right, cross a bridge over a main road and immediately turn left, at a public bridleway sign, along a fence-lined track parallel to the road. At a public footpath sign, turn right through a kissing-gate **H** and walk along an enclosed path, later continuing along the left-hand edge of a field.

In the field corner, bear left to go through a kissing-gate that admits you to Beverley Westwood, a huge area of open common land to the west of the town. Turn right along the right-hand edge of the common **J** and continue by its right-hand edge, heading down into a dip and up again, to reach the corner. Turn left alongside a fence parallel to a road and continue along the road towards one of several windmills on the common. Take the first road on the left **K** and follow it gently downhill across Westwood, enjoying superb views to the right of the west front of Beverley Minster and the Holderness plain beyond.

After going through gates on the edge of the common, continue along Westwood Road and then along Newbegin to a T-junction. Keep ahead along an alley into Saturday Market. ●

Beverley from Westwood

Pocklington Canal and Allerthorpe Common

Start	Pocklington
Distance	9½ miles (15.3km)
Approximate time	4½ hours
Parking	Pocklington
Refreshments	Pubs and cafés at Pocklington, pub at Canal Head, pub at Allerthorpe
Ordnance Survey maps	Landranger 106 (Market Weighton), Explorer 294 (Market Weighton & Yorkshire Wolds Central)

Although lengthy, this is an entirely flat route in the Vale of York below the western slopes of the wolds. Much of the first part is beside the disused Pocklington Canal. Then comes a stretch along quiet lanes, followed by a walk through the delightful woodlands of Allerthorpe Common. There are attractive and extensive views over the vale to the line of the wolds.

The pleasant old town of Pocklington is situated near the eastern edge of the Vale of York below the western escarpment of the wolds. Its fine medieval church, just off the Market Place, has an imposing 15th-century tower.

The walk starts in the Market Place. Turn down Railway Street to a crossroads, keep ahead (still along Railway Street) and after ½ mile (800m) turn left **A** along a lane signposted to 'Pocklington Canal Picnic Site'. At a T-junction turn left and at a public bridleway sign opposite The Wellington Oak public house, turn right **B** along a tarmac track through the Canal Head picnic area. Pass beside a gate and continue along a pleasant, partially tree-lined path beside the Pocklington Canal for almost two miles (3.2km). The canal was constructed between 1815 and 1818 to link Pocklington with the River Derwent and the industrialised parts of Yorkshire. It fell into disuse and has been partially restored, although the bed is choked with vegetation and little water can be seen.

At the first road bridge, where the path emerges onto a lane, turn right **C** along the narrow lane to a T-junction. Turn left along a road, take the first lane on the right **D**, signposted to Thornton, and follow it into the village, passing to the right of the small medieval church. Beyond the village, turn right along the lane signposted to Sutton on Derwent **E** and, after one mile (1.6km), turn right at a public footpath sign **F**, along a track that keeps by the right-hand edge of a field.

On entering the next field, the track curves left towards a barn and then bears right to keep along the right-hand edge of the woodland of Allerthorpe Common. Where the track bends right, turn left into the trees to a T-junction,

"

turn right and continue along a path that keeps close to the right-hand edge of the woodland, a most attractive part of the walk. After bearing right and passing beside a gate, continue through more woodland (Tank Plantation), eventually emerging from the trees onto a track. Ahead is a fine view of the wolds.

Follow the track to a farm, after which it emerges onto a lane, and keep ahead to a T-junction. Turn right and, at the next T-junction by the Plough Inn, turn left G along a road through Allerthorpe, a pleasant village with

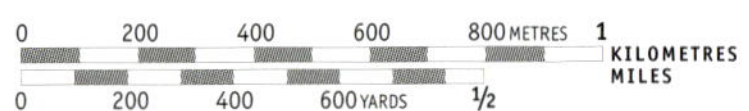

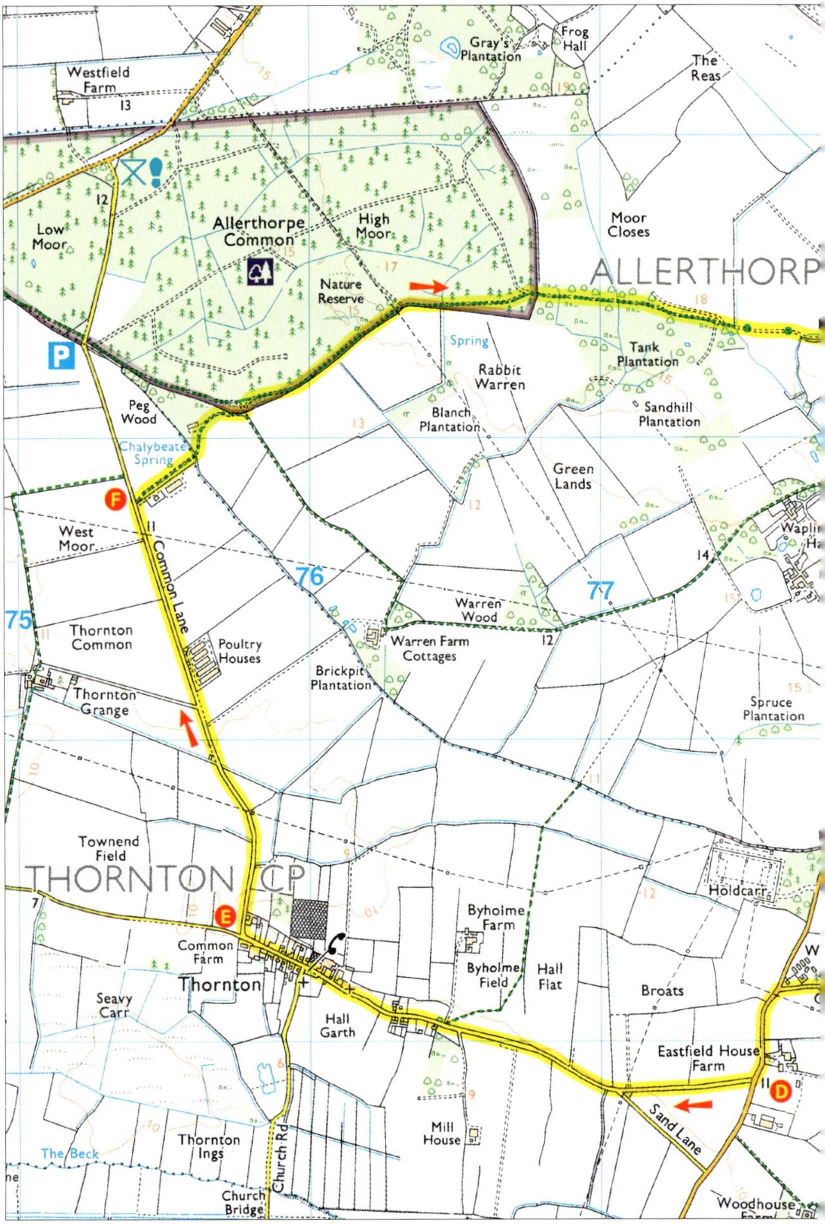

SCALE 1:25 000 or 2½ INCHES to 1 MILE 4CM to 1KM

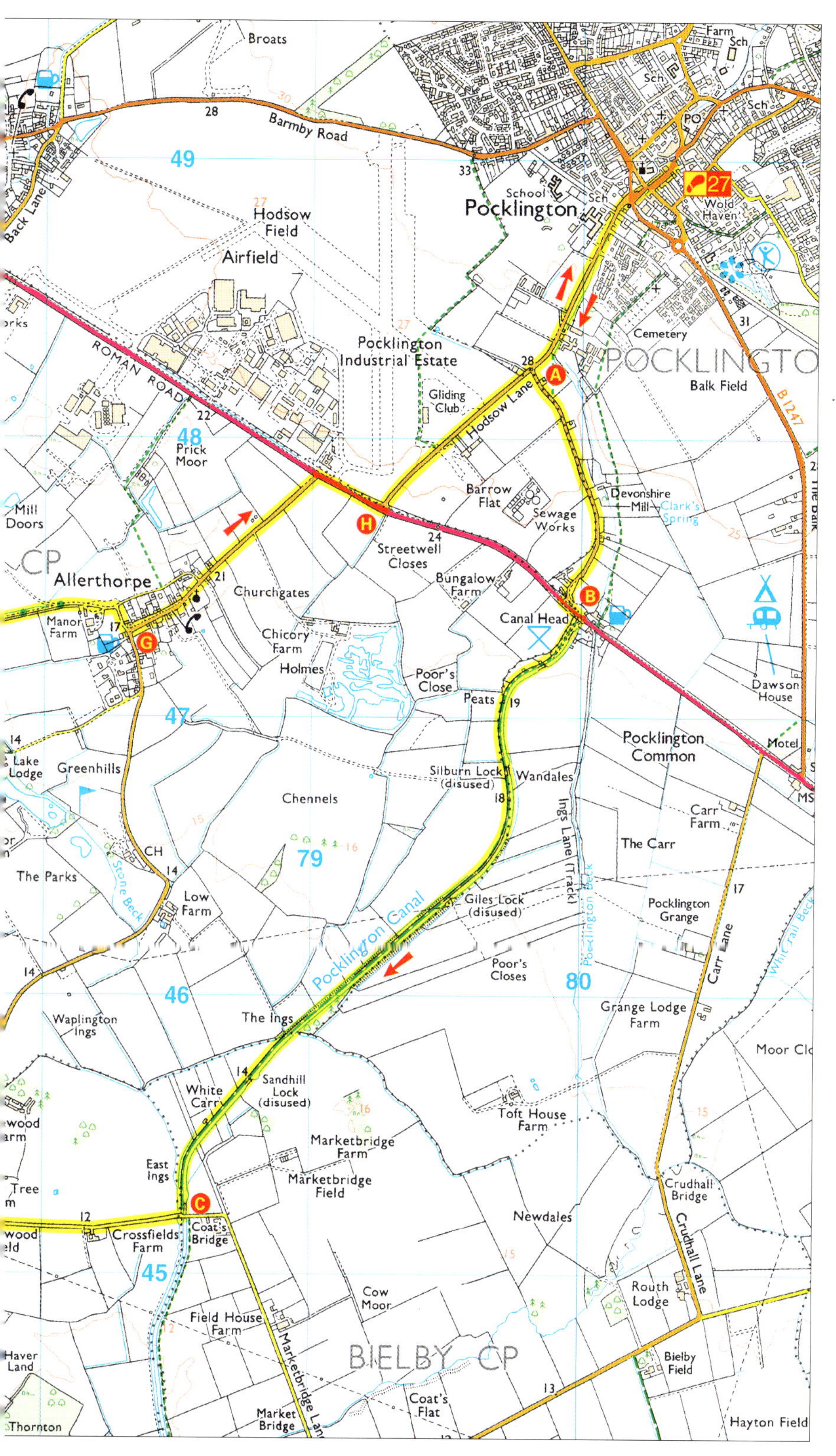

Broats
Barmby Road
28
30
49
33
School
Pocklington
Sch
Sch
Sch
PO
Sch'
Farm
Sch
27
Wold Haven
Hodsow Field
Airfield
27
Cemetery
31
POCKLINGTO
ROMAN ROAD
Pocklington Industrial Estate
28
A
Hodsow Lane
Balk Field
B 1247
22
48
Prick Moor
Gliding Club
Barrow Flat
Sewage Works
Devonshire Mill
Clark's Spring
25
Mill Doors
H
24
Streetwell Closes
Bungalow Farm
CP
Allerthorpe
21
Churchgates
B
Canal Head
Manor Farm
17
G
Chicory Farm
Holmes
Poor's Close
Peats
19
Pocklington Common
Dawson House
Motel
47
14
Lake Lodge
Greenhills
Silburn Lock (disused)
Wandales
18
Carr Farm
The Carr
Chennels
15
16
79
Ings Lane (Track)
Pocklington Beck
Pocklington Grange
17
CH
14
The Parks
Stone Beck
Low Farm
Giles Lock (disused)
Pocklington Canal
46
14
Poor's Closes
80
Grange Lodge Farm
Whitfall Beck
Carr Lane
Moor Clo
Waplington Ings
The Ings
14
White Carr
Sandhill Lock (disused)
16
Toft House Farm
15
wood arm
East Ings
Marketbridge Farm
Marketbridge Field
Newdales
Crudhall Bridge
Crudhall Lane
Tree m
C
Coat's Bridge
wood eld
12
Crossfields Farm
45
Routh Lodge
Field House Farm
Cow Moor
Bielby Field
Haver Land
BIELBY CP
13
Thornton
Market Bridge
Marketbridge Lane
Coat's Flat
Hayton Field

Pocklington Canal

wide verges lined by old cottages. Pass to the left of the small Victorian church and continue along the road to a T-junction.

Cross the main road, taking care as it is busy, and turn right – there is a path beside the road. Take the first road on the left **H**, signposted to Pocklington, which leads back to the starting point of the walk.

Thixendale and Kirby Underdale

Start	Thixendale
Distance	8 miles (12.9km)
Approximate time	4 hours
Parking	Roadside parking at Thixendale
Refreshments	Pub and café at Thixendale
Ordnance Survey maps	Landrangers 100 (Malton & Pickering) and 106 (Market Weighton), Explorers 294 (Market Weighton & Yorkshire Wolds Central) and 300 (Howardian Hills & Malton)

This reasonably energetic walk takes you across some of the quietest and loneliest country of the Yorkshire Wolds. The first and last parts are through the steep-sided Thixen Dale and adjacent dales, some of the dry valleys that are characteristic of the chalk country of the wolds. In between, the route passes through the attractive village of Kirby Underdale. There are some superb views from the western edge of the wolds, looking across the wide expanses of the Vale of York.

Start by facing the church, turn right and where the lane curves right, keep ahead through a gate **A** at a public bridleway sign. At a fork, take the left-hand track through Thixen Dale, climbing several stiles. Where the dale forks, bear right through a gate and continue through Milham Dale.

At a fork, take the left-hand, lower track, which continues gently up towards the head of the dale and, on joining a track, bear right up to a gate. Go through and at a T-junction, turn left along a track to a road **B**. Turn left and, after almost $\frac{1}{2}$ mile (800m), turn right **C** at a public footpath sign (which is on the opposite side of the road), along the right-hand edge of a field, heading downhill. Ahead is a superb view over the Vale of York.

At a T-junction in a field corner, turn left along a track and, in the next corner, turn right over a stile and head downhill, by a line of trees on the left, to a stile. Climb it, continue downhill along the left-hand edge of a field and, in the bottom corner, pass between redundant gateposts and turn left along the left-hand edge of the next field. Follow the field edge to the right, continue downhill along its left-hand edge and, about 50 yds (46m) before reaching the corner, look out for where a yellow waymark directs you to turn left onto a grassy track by the right-hand edge of a field.

In the next field you join a well-surfaced track and follow this winding and undulating track to a lane **D**. Turn right downhill, follow the lane around a

Looking over the Vale of York from the wolds near Thixendale

left-hand bend and, at a T-junction, turn left into the delightful hamlet of Kirby Underdale. Follow the lane around a left-hand bend and head down into a dip, passing to the right of the attractive and interesting church, a superb example of a Norman village church. Continue along the lane and, just after a left-hand bend, turn right over a stile **E** at a public footpath sign and walk straight across a field – Painsthorpe Hall is to the left – heading

up to a gate on the far side. Go through the gate and then turn left along a track, which curves right and keeps to the left of a farm to emerge onto a narrow lane.

Keep ahead to a T-junction – here rejoining the previous lane – turn right and continue steadily uphill to a T-junction on the crest. Turn left, at a public bridleway sign turn right **F** along a track, pass to the right of farm buildings and continue along the straight track. At a waymarked post, follow the track around a left-hand bend and, where it bends right, keep ahead along the left-hand edge of a field. After passing through a gap, turn right along the right-hand edge of the next field, heading gently downhill to a gate. Go through, keep ahead in the same direction across rough pasture, keep to the left of a fence corner and descend into the steep-sided and narrow Worm Dale.

At the bottom, bear right to continue through the dale to a gate and go through to where Worm Dale emerges into Thixen Dale **G**. Turn left and, at a fork and footpath post, take the left-hand path – here joining the Wolds Way – to continue through the dale, negotiating several stiles and gates. On emerging onto a lane **H**, turn right into Thixendale village and turn left along the lane, signposted to Birdsall and Malton, to return to the starting point of the walk.

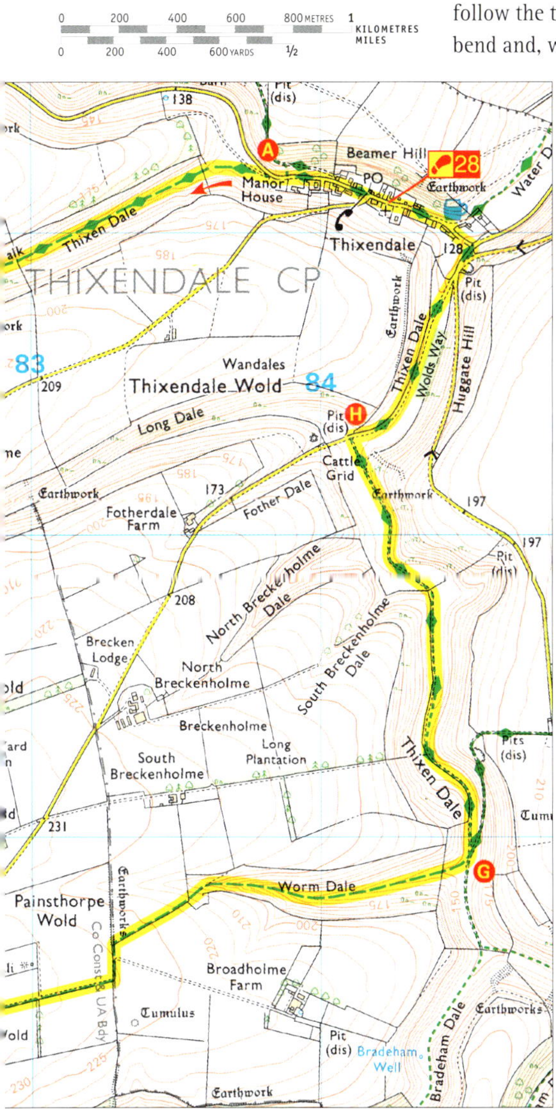

Further Information

The National Trust

Anyone who likes visiting places of natural beauty and/or historic interest has cause to be grateful to the National Trust. Without it, many such places would probably have vanished by now.

It was in response to the pressures on the countryside posed by the relentless march of Victorian industrialisation that the trust was set up in 1895. Its founders, inspired by the common goals of protecting and conserving Britain's national heritage and widening public access to it, were Sir Robert Hunter, Octavia Hill and Canon Rawnsley: respectively a solicitor, a social reformer and a clergyman. The latter was particularly influential. As a canon of Carlisle Cathedral and vicar of Crosthwaite (near Keswick), he was concerned about threats to the Lake District and had already been active in protecting footpaths and promoting public access to open countryside. After the flooding of Thirlmere in 1879 to create a large reservoir, he became increasingly convinced that the only effective way to guarantee protection was outright ownership of land.

The purpose of the National Trust is to preserve areas of natural beauty and sites of historic interest by acquisition, holding them in trust for the nation and making them available for public access and enjoyment. Some of its properties have been acquired through purchase, but many of the Trust's properties have been donated. Nowadays it is not only one of the biggest landowners in the country, but also one of the most active conservation charities, protecting 581,113 acres (253,176 ha) of land, including 555 miles (892km) of coastline, and over 300 historic properties in England, Wales and Northern Ireland. (There is a separate National Trust for Scotland, which was set up in 1931.)

Furthermore, once a piece of land has come under National Trust ownership, it is difficult for its status to be altered. As a result of parliamentary legislation in 1907, the Trust was given the right to declare its property inalienable, so ensuring that in any subsequent dispute it can appeal directly to parliament.

As it works towards its dual aims of conserving areas of attractive countryside and encouraging greater public access (not easy to reconcile in this age of mass tourism), the Trust provides an excellent service for walkers by creating new concessionary paths and waymarked trails, maintaining stiles and foot bridges and combating the ever-increasing problem of footpath erosion.

For details of membership, contact the National Trust at the address on page 95.

The Ramblers' Association

No organisation works more actively to protect and extend the rights and interests of walkers in the countryside than the Ramblers' Association. Its aims are clear: to foster a greater knowledge, love and care of the countryside; to assist in the protection and enhancement of public rights of way and areas of natural beauty; to work for greater public access to the countryside; and to encourage more people to take up rambling as a healthy, recreational leisure activity.

It was founded in 1935 when, following the setting up of a National Council of Ramblers' Federations in 1931, a number of federations earlier formed in London, Manchester, the Midlands and elsewhere came together to create a more effective pressure group, to deal with such problems as the disappearance and obstruction of footpaths, the prevention of access to open mountain and moorland and increasing hostility from landowners. This was the era of the mass trespasses, when there were sometimes violent

Devil's Arrows, Boroughbridge

confrontations between ramblers and gamekeepers, especially on the moorlands of the Peak District.

Since then the Ramblers' Association has played an influential role in preserving and developing the national footpath network, supporting the creation of national parks and encouraging the designation and waymarking of long-distance routes.

Our freedom to walk in the countryside is precarious and requires constant vigilance. As well as the perennial problems of footpaths being illegally obstructed, disappearing through lack of use or extinguished by housing or road construction, new dangers can spring up at any time.

It is to meet such problems and dangers that the Ramblers' Association exists and represents the interests of all walkers. The address to write to for information on the Ramblers' Association and how to become a member is given on page 95.

 ## Walkers and the Law

The average walker in a national park or other popular walking area, armed with the appropriate Ordnance Survey map, reinforced perhaps by a guidebook giving detailed walking instructions, is unlikely to run into legal difficulties, but it is useful to know something about the law relating to public rights of way. The right to walk over certain parts of the countryside has developed over a long period, and how such rights came into being is a complex subject, too lengthy to be discussed here. The following comments are intended simply as a helpful guide, backed up by the Countryside Access Charter, a concise summary of walkers' rights and obligations drawn up by the Countryside Agency (see page 94).

Basically there are two main kinds of public rights of way: footpaths (for walkers only) and bridleways (for walkers, riders on horseback and pedal cyclists). Footpaths and bridleways are shown by broken green lines on Ordnance Survey Explorer maps and broken red lines on Landranger maps. There is also a third category, called byways: chiefly broad tracks (green lanes) or farm roads, which walkers, riders and cyclists have to share, usually only occasionally, with motor vehicles. Many of these public paths have been in existence for hundreds of years and some even originated as prehistoric trackways and have been in constant use for well over 2,000 years. Ways known as RUPPs (roads used as public paths) still appear on some maps. The legal definition of such byways is ambiguous and they are gradually being reclassified as footpaths, bridleways or byways.

The term 'right of way' means exactly what it says. It gives right of passage over what, in the vast majority of cases, is private land, and you are required to keep to the line of the path and not stray on to the land on either side. If you inadvertently wander off the right of way – either because of faulty map-reading or because the route is not clearly indicated on the ground – you are technically trespassing and the wisest course is to ask the nearest available person (farmer or fellow walker) to direct you back to the correct route. There are stories about unpleasant confrontations between walkers and farmers at times, but in general most farmers are co-operative when responding to a genuine and polite request for assistance in route-finding.

Obstructions can sometimes be a problem and probably the most common of these is where a path across a field has been ploughed up. It is legal for a farmer to plough up a path provided that he restores it within two weeks, barring exceptionally bad weather. This does not always happen and here the walker is presented with a dilemma: to follow the line of the path, even if this inevitably means treading on crops, or to walk around the edge of the field. The latter course of action often seems the best but this means that you would be trespassing and not keeping to the exact line of the path. In the case of other obstructions which may block a path (illegal fences and locked gates etc), common sense has to be used in order to negotiate them by the easiest method – detour or removal. You should only ever remove as much as is necessary to get through, and if you can easily go round the obstruction without causing any damage, then you should do so. If you have any problems negotiating rights of way, you should report the matter to the rights of way department of the relevant council, which will take action with the landowner concerned.

Apart from rights of way enshrined by law, there are a number of other paths available to walkers. Permissive or concessionary paths have been created where a landowner has given permission for the public to use a particular route across his land. The main problem with these is that, as they have been granted as a concession, there is no legal right to use them and therefore they can be extinguished at any time. In practice, many of these concessionary routes have been established on land owned either by large public bodies such as the Forestry Commission, or by a private one, such as the National Trust, and as these mainly encourage walkers to use their paths, they are unlikely to be closed unless a change of ownership occurs.

Filey

Countryside Access Charter

Your rights of way are:

- public footpaths – on foot only. Sometimes waymarked in yellow
- bridle-ways – on foot, horseback and pedal cycle. Sometimes waymarked in blue
- byways (usually old roads), most 'roads used as public paths' and, of course, public roads – all traffic has the right of way

Use maps, signs and waymarks to check rights of way. Ordnance Survey Explorer and Landranger maps show most public rights of way

On rights of way you can:

- take a pram, pushchair or wheelchair if practicable
- take a dog (on a lead or under close control)
- take a short route round an illegal obstruction or remove it sufficiently to get past

You have a right to go for recreation to:

- public parks and open spaces – on foot
- most commons near older towns and cities – on foot and sometimes on horseback
- private land where the owner has a formal agreement with the local authority

In addition you can use the following by local or established custom or consent, but ask for advice if you are unsure:

- many areas of open country, such as moorland, fell and coastal areas, especially those in the care of the National Trust, and some commons
- some woods and forests, especially those owned by the Forestry Commission
- country parks and picnic sites
- most beaches
- canal towpaths
- some private paths and tracks Consent sometimes extends to horse-riding and cycling

For your information:

- county councils and London boroughs maintain and record rights of way, and register commons
- obstructions, dangerous animals, harassment and misleading signs on rights of way are illegal and you should report them to the county council
- paths across fields can be ploughed, but must normally be reinstated within two weeks
- landowners can require you to leave land to which you have no right of access
- motor vehicles are normally permitted only on roads, byways and some 'roads used as public paths'

Walkers also have free access to country parks (except where requested to keep away from certain areas for eco-logical reasons, e.g wildlife protection, woodland regeneration, etc), canal tow-paths and most beaches. By custom, though not by right, you are generally free to walk across the open and uncultivated higher land of mountain, moorland and fell, but this varies from area to area and from one season to another – grouse moors, for example, will be out of bounds during the breeding and shooting seasons and some open areas are used as Ministry of Defence firing ranges, for which reason access will be restricted. In some areas the situation has been clarified as a result of 'access agreements' between the land-owners and either the county council or the national park authority, which clearly define when and where you can walk over such open country.

Walking Safety

Although the reasonably gentle countryside that is the subject of this book offers no real dangers to walkers at any time of the year, it is still advisable to take sensible precautions and follow certain well-tried guidelines.

Always take with you both warm and waterproof clothing and sufficient food and drink. Wear suitable footwear, such as strong walking boots or shoes that give a good grip over stony ground, on slippery slopes and in muddy conditions. Try to obtain a local weather forecast and bear it in mind before you start. Do not be afraid to abandon your proposed route and return to your starting point in the event of a sudden and unexpected deterioration in the weather.

All the walks described in this book will be safe to do, given due care and respect, even during the winter. Indeed, a crisp, fine winter day often provides perfect walking conditions, with firm ground underfoot and a clarity unique to this time of the year. The most difficult hazard likely to be encountered is mud, especially when walking along woodland and field paths, farm tracks and bridleways – the latter in particular can often get churned up by cyclists and horses. In summer, an additional difficulty may be narrow and overgrown paths, particularly along the edges of cultivated fields. Neither should constitute a major problem provided that the appropriate footwear is worn.

Useful Organisations

Campaign to Protect Rural England
128 Southwark Street,
London SE1 OSW
Tel. 020 7981 2800
www.cpre.org.uk

Tithe Barn at Nether Poppleton

Countryside Agency
John Dower House,
Crescent Place, Cheltenham,
Gloucestershire GL50 3RA
Tel. 01242 521381
www.countryside.gov.uk

East Riding of Yorkshire County Council
County Hall, Beverley HU17 9BA
Tel. 01482 887700

Forestry Commission
Silvan House, 231 Corstorphine Road,
Edinburgh EH12 7AT
Tel. 0131 334 0303

Long Distance Walkers' Association
Bank House, High Street, Wrotham,
Sevenoaks, Kent TN15 7AE
Tel. 01732 883705

National Trust
Membership and general enquiries:
PO Box 39, Warrington WA5 7WD
Tel. 0870 458 4000

Yorkshire Regional Office:
Goddards, 27 Tadcaster Road,
Dringhouses, York YO24 1GG
Tel. 01904 702021
North Yorkshire County Council
County Hall, Northallerton
DL7 8AD
Tel. 01609 780780

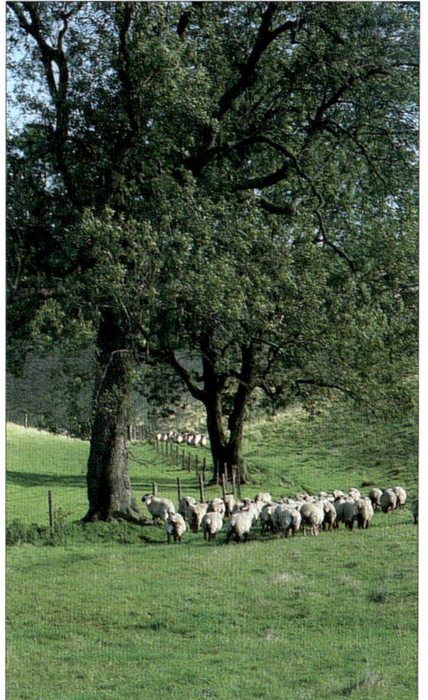

Sheep in Horse Dale

Ordnance Survey
Romsey Road, Maybush,
Southampton SO16 4GU
Tel. 08456 05 05 05 (Lo-call)

Ramblers' Association
2nd Floor, Camelford House,
87–90 Albert Embankment,
London SE1 7TW
Tel. 020 7339 8500

Yorkshire Tourist Board,
312 Tadcaster Road,
York YO24 1GS
Tel. 0870 609 0000

Tourist Information Centres
*(*not open all year):*
Beverley: 01482 391672
Bridlington: 01262 673474
*Easingwold: 01347 821530
*Filey: 01723 383636
Kingston upon Hull: 01482 223559
Malton: 01653 600048
Northallerton: 01609 776864
*Ripon: 01765 604625
*Thirsk: 01845 522755
York: 01904 621756

Youth Hostels Association
Trevelyan House,
Dimple Road,
Matlock, Derbyshire
DE4 3YH
Tel. 01629 592600
www.yha.org.uk

 *Ordnance Survey maps of the Vale of York and the Yorkshire Wolds*

The area of the Vale of York and the Yorkshire Wolds is covered by Ordnance Survey 1:50 000 ($1\frac{1}{4}$ inches to 1 mile or 2cm to 1km) scale Landranger map sheets 99, 100, 101, 105, 106 and 107. These all-purpose maps are packed with information to help you explore the area. Viewpoints, picnic sites, places of interest and caravan and camping sites are shown, as well as public rights of way information such as footpaths and bridleways.

To examine the area in more detail and especially if you are planning walks, Ordnance Survey Explorer maps at 1:25 000 ($2\frac{1}{2}$ inches to 1 mile or 4cm to 1km) scale are ideal:

289 Leeds
290 York
291 Goole & Gilberdyke
292 Withernsea & Spurn Head
293 Kingston upon Hill & Beverley
294 Market Weighton & Yorkshire Wolds Central
295 Bridlington, Driffield & Hornsea
299 Ripon & Boroughbridge
300 Howardian Hills & Malton
301 Scarborough, Bridlington & Flamborough Head

To get to the Vale of York, use the Ordnance Survey OS Travel Map-Road 4 (Northern England) at 1:250 000 scale (1cm to 2.5km or 1 inch to 4 miles) or the OS Travel Map-Route Great Britain at 1:625 000 scale (4cm to 25km or 1 inch to 10 miles).

Ordnance Survey maps and guides are available from most booksellers, stationers and newsagents.

www.totalwalking.co.uk

www.totalwalking.co.uk
is the official website of the Jarrold
Pathfinder and Short Walks guides. This
interactive website features a wealth of
information for walkers – from the latest
news on route diversions and advice from
professional walkers to product news, free
sample walks and promotional offers.

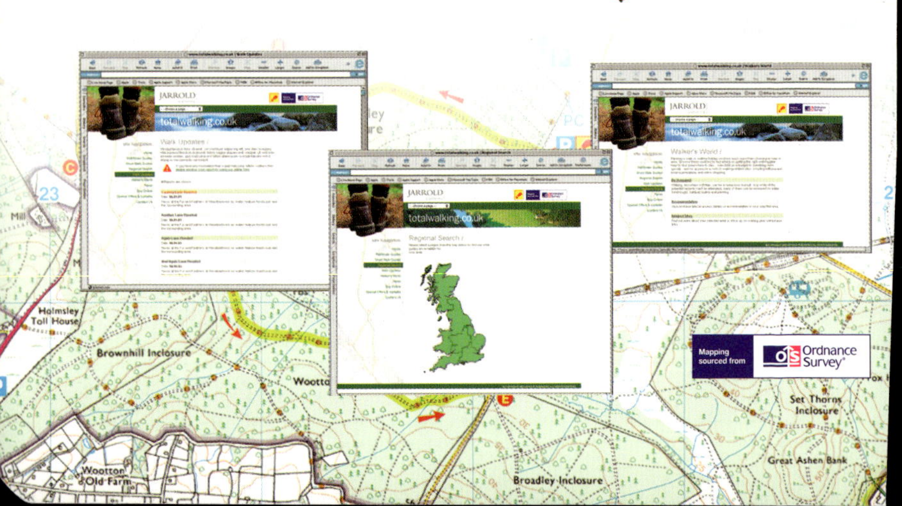